Oops,
Your
Manners
Are
Showing™

A Study Course for Ages 8 & Up
Second Edition, Second Printing

Peggy Norwood & Jan Stabler

Teacher's Edition

Published by The Oops Group
P. O. Box 5868
Katy, Texas 77491

Illustrated by Andrea Barth and Tera Yoshimura

Printed in the United States of America

PREFACE

"Are you teaching the manners class this spring?" an eager parent asks. "I try to talk to my children about manners, but they have to hear about it from someone else, or they just won't believe it."

Another parent who talks about her children's manners laughs and says, "Work is needed."

A private school teacher says, "We asked parents what subjects they wanted included in our curriculum. Many asked us to teach manners. I'm confused with some of the rules myself. I'm looking for a really good source of information."

We meet many eager parents who want their children to learn good manners. Many children, however, are less than eager to enroll in a course about manners. They expect such a class to be B-O-R-I-N-G. On the other hand, some children are anxious to have manners explained to them and have a chance to practice. We were challenged to design a manners course that would attract children at all levels of interest while teaching them how to be considerate of others.

We are no strangers to challenge. We have served as teachers and directors in Sunday School, VBS, mission projects, and special events for thirty combined years. We began serving together when we co-directed our church's Vacation Bible School and wrote a great deal of the VBS program. Since then, we have been challenged by many exciting joint projects in children's ministry.

Anxious to meet the challenge of teaching children the importance of manners, we thoroughly researched the subject as we strived to develop an enjoyable, positive, and motivating course. This course functions as a workshop with many opportunities for practice. Children enjoy all the activities, which include drama, team building, role playing, games, word puzzles, and the ever popular food-sampling.

Lessons are interwoven through each of the activities. For example, students act as good citizens by donating canned food to a food bank after using the cans in the table manners study. In addition, the frequent Scriptural references heighten the students' awareness of God's pleasure in our consideration of others and the importance of looking to God's Word for direction.

Furthermore, parents say they see learning and practicing good manners as an ongoing process. This course not only sets the process in motion, but it also teaches the students how to continue learning by using and adding to their workbooks. Another resource is "Manners to Grow On," a special section in the student workbook that will be valuable as the students grow in grace and knowledge.

It is exciting to watch children grow through this course. Many of the students name the course as a favorite, even thanking their parents for enrolling them. Parents say, "Things are going a lot better around our house now that my child is taking the course. We are all learning."

This Teacher's Edition offers others the opportunity to teach the course and impact households. The easy-to-follow lesson plans guide the teacher through each of the lessons.

Skits, copy sheets, supply lists, and answers to word games also comprise this Teacher's Edition. All of these aids have been used successfully in both small and large groups. We have designed this study as a good source of information as well as an entertaining and practical course for both students and teachers.

In answer to parents and teachers, we say, "You really can teach your children manners." Children quickly become "hooked" on the idea that showing consideration of others is exciting. If parents and teachers are not careful, they also may be gently reminded to put others first.

Peggy Norwood
Jan Stabler

HOW TO USE THIS STUDY COURSE

Learning about the Course

- **"Course Overview"** on page 5 helps you plan your course. The course is divided into eight lessons and may be taught in eight weeks or for a longer or shorter period by dividing the material to accommodate your time period. Class material may be taught at a steady pace within one hour to an hour and fifteen minutes. Allow more time for practice when teaching a class of younger students.

- **"What's Your Format?"** on pages 6 - 8 explains the optional class settings in which this course may be taught . . . to one student, with a few students, or in the classroom.

- Each class has a **step-by-step lesson plan** with words in **bold** that may be said verbatim or paraphrased during the class.

- During class, the teacher asks the students to turn to page numbers in their workbooks to help them become familiar with the lessons. "T.Ed." included after a page number listed in the lesson plans refers to a page in the **Teacher's Edition**.

- **Copy sheets** beginning on page 106 help to customize and enhance the course. The copy sheets are easy to understand and to use. The explanation for all copy sheets is listed first. Then the individual copy sheets follow in numerical order.

Preparing for the Course

- **Select** your format and **invite** students to enroll in your study course.

- **Purchase** a workbook for each student enrolled.

- Read the **student workbook** to become familiar with the lessons. Teach, however, from the lesson plans which contain all the information needed.

- Before studying the lesson plans for each class, read **"Teaching Materials Overview"** and **"Teaching Materials"** for the class.

- Study the **lesson plans** as you prepare for each class and gather the **teaching materials**. Parents may be able to assist in gathering materials.

TABLE OF CONTENTS

Course Overview

The students follow the adventures of Wilhelminanina Oopsman (Oops or Oopsy to her friends). In the first skit, Oops's manners are showing. . . room for improvement. Despite Oops's objections, her mother enthusiastically enrolls her in a manners class. Through skits, cartoons, and examples in the lessons, Oops's good manners begin to show. She interacts with friends and family members listed in the Cast of Characters on page 94.

CLASS	LESSON	TABLE SETTING	FOOD SERVED	SKIT
1	Courtesy Begins at Home	Getting Down to Basics	Option: Pudding or applesauce	"Meet Oops"
2	Introductions	Give Us Our Daily Bread	Bread/butter	"Oops Skips the Introductions"
3	Conversation	Beverages	Mints; soft drink or fruit juice	"Mini Mint Skit" & "Excuse Me"
4	Telephone Etiquette	Is It Soup Yet?	Soup crackers	"Rose Is Invited"
5	Guest Relations	Salad/Napkins	Cake/punch	
6	Manners Away from Home	Five Course Setting	Popcorn, peanuts, chips, or pretzels	
7	Table Manners	Dinner Is Served	Appetizer	"Lunch with Mamaw" & "Oops at the Table"
8	Thank You Notes; Serving; Night Out	Finger Bowl and Dessert	Dessert/drink	

WHAT'S YOUR FORMAT?

There are as many options as there are opportunities and situations in which to teach this course. Examples are church related activities, supplements for Scriptural study and character building, evening classes, after school classes, extra curricular programs, home lessons, unit studies, co-op groups, activity day programs, and community workshops.

One Student

Teacher

- One teacher or self-taught

Lesson Plans

- The step-by-step lesson plans direct the study course through the classroom format; however, *sentences in italics throughout the lesson plans suggest ways to adapt the lessons for one or a few students.*

- Identify areas that are of special interest or that need special attention. Focus more study time with the student in these areas. Option: Alter the order of the lessons if needed to better serve the student and your program. Note: The answers to each word game and the Scripture verse review are in the lesson that follows the game and the verse.

- Share your experiences and insights with the student. Help the student to apply the lessons to his own life.

- **Skits:** One student reads the skits, performs with the teacher, or invites others to participate. You may need to change female characters in the skits to male characters; for example, change Mom's role to Dad's and Rose Valentine's to her husband's (Moses). In this case, instead of Mom's offering Rose a cup of coffee in the "Meet Oops" Skit, Dad offers to show Moses his power tools.

Keeping Score

- Assist the student in marking his points earned on the score sheets. See explanation of Copy Sheet # 1, page 106.

- The student serves his family a meal to demonstrate what he has learned.

- Consider planning a night out with the student at a restaurant.

6

A Few Students

Teacher

- One teacher

Lesson Plans

- The step-by-step lesson plans direct the study course through the classroom format; however, *sentences in italics throughout the lesson plans suggest ways to adapt the lesson for one or a few students.*

- Identify areas that are of special interest or that need special attention. Focus more study time in these areas with the students. Option: Alter the order of the lessons if needed to better serve your students and your program. Note: The answers to each word game and the Scripture verse review are in the lesson that follows the game and the verse.

- Share your experiences and insights with your students.

- **Skits:** See this topic for "One Student."

Keeping Score

- Keep a separate folder with score sheets. See explanation of Copy Sheet # 1, page 106. Students may also want to circle points in their folders.

- A party is planned for the last class. (See "Just Desserts Cafe," page 90.) The student with the most points is served refreshments by one or two students. With four or more students, divide as evenly as possible the number of students to serve and be served. The party can be an enjoyable learning experience for all the students. Option: Invite friends and family to the party.

- Consider planning a night out with the students at a restaurant.

Classroom

Teachers

- One or two lead teachers *or* several teachers taking responsibility for leading in different lessons.

Lesson Plans

- Step-by-step lesson plans direct the study course through the classroom format. *Sentences in italics throughout the lesson plans suggest ways to adapt lessons for one or a few students.* Some of the suggestions may be helpful in the classroom.

- Option: Alter the order of the lessons if needed to better serve your students and your program. Note: Answers to each word game and the review of the Scripture verse are in the lesson that follows the game and the verse. When making this change, also alter Copy Sheet # 2.

- Share your experiences and insights with the students during the lessons.

Teams

- Forming teams teaches friendly competition. The team members have a chance to practice the lessons while building camaraderie and learning about team work.

- Assign each student to a team. For each team, choose a team color. Assign each team to a table.

- Prepare a team folder (in the team color) for each team. See how to assemble on page 9, "Teaching Materials Overview." Place the folder on the team's table.

Team Leaders

- Adults serve as team leaders ("Guidelines for Team Leaders," Copy Sheet # 2).

- Team leaders sit with the team. During "Team Time" at the beginning of class, leaders circle team points that the students earn, and they assist in activities.

Without Team Leaders

- One or two lead teachers (or students) fulfill the duties of the team leaders. Allow adequate time for teachers to work with each team.

- During "Team Time," teams waiting for teachers may eat the snack, make a craft, make bookmarks for the Bible verses, work the word games, listen to each other's memory verses, practice the table setting, look up the reference verses in the Bible, and write a paragraph or story on related topics.

Team Scores

- Team leaders circle points for each student on the score sheets in the team folder. See explanation of Copy Sheet # 1, page 106 for further information.

- Total the scores for each team and post them before class. Average the totals if the number of students on the teams are uneven.

- The team with fewer team points serves refreshments to the team with more team points at the last class. (See "Just Desserts Cafe," page 90.)

8 ~ What's Your Format? ~

Copyright © 1997 The Oops Group. Not to be reproduced.

TEACHING MATERIALS OVERVIEW

Materials in the Classroom

Set up a table and chairs for each team. Allow space for seating of students and team leaders, students' workbooks, food, and displays.

Provide a table and chair in front of the class for yourself and your teaching materials, a table near the classroom door for the "Entry Display," and a table and chair located to the side for "Teaching the Table Setting." In the case of limited tables, use the teacher's table or the "Entry Display" Table for "Teaching the Table Setting." Allow space at the front of the classroom for performing skits and practicing the lessons.

Set up a chalk or dry eraser board. Keep a carry-all for teaching materials.

Materials for All Classes

- ❏ Teacher's Edition
- ❏ team folders in team colors (Use folders with pockets & brads. See below how to assemble. Place each team's folder on the team's table before class.)
- ❏ pencil box with pencils for students & team leaders, & glue sticks for the teams' tables (Place pencils & glue sticks at each team's table.)
- ❏ chalk or markers
- ❏ manners articles that students bring to class (A student pastes each article to a sheet of paper.) Punch holes for the student's folder and summarize the articles at the end of the following class or ask the student to tell about the article.
- ❏ container for completed "Good Manners Report Cards" & manners articles that students bring to class
- ❏ updated team scores (Post scores before each class.)

Materials for Each Class

Materials are listed for each class beginning on page 11. Parents may be able to help gather the supplies.

Materials in Each Team Folder

- ❏ Table Label: folded card stock in team color with team name (team selects name at Class 1) Place a Table Label on each team's table.
- ❏ set of score sheets per student (See explanation of Copy Sheet # 1, page 106.)
- ❏ "Guidelines for Team Leaders" (See explanation of Copy Sheet # 2, page 106.)
- ❏ "Good Manners Report Cards" (See explanation of Copy Sheet # 5, page 107.)

Entry Display

Create a more inviting classroom by adding some displays and decorative touches on a table at the entry to the classroom. Arrange items on hand that relate to the lesson. For Classes 1 and 2, make a "manners" poster or foam board display with pictures or items that relate to manners. *One or a few students help make the poster display. Use the poster as a review after the conclusion of the course.*

Arrange a basic setting near the poster as part of your display. Refer to "Getting Down to Basics," pages 94 - 95.

Teaching the Table Setting

■ Students learn the basic table setting during the first class and add pieces at each class. Students set the basic table setting at each class before learning about new pieces.

■ Each lesson plan gives a summary of the table setting information to be taught in each class. Refer to "Set for Success," beginning on page 94, for complete information.

■ During "Team Time" activities, teach the table setting lesson to one team at a time, giving each student the opportunity to practice. (Assign teams in the same order each class.) *One or a few students practice at the same time.*

■ Using china, glassware, and silverware for students to practice the table setting contributes to the interest and value of the lessons. The sets you use, however, may be everyday dinnerware and stainless silverware.

Poster Board Place Setting

Preparation

Cut large shapes of a place setting from brightly colored poster board. Refer to "Set for Success," page 95 as a guide. Outline the pieces with a black marker to give the appearance of depth. Option: Cut white paper or poster board. Spray silver or gold paint on silverware shapes; draw a pattern on the dinnerware and glassware shapes; use fabric for the napkin shape. Laminate pieces and add velcro to the backs. Option: *One or a few students make the pieces.*

Usage

Students hold pieces and "arrange themselves" or arrange pieces on felt board.

Purpose

This optional teaching aid adds excitement to the course. Introduce the poster place setting for the table manners lesson in Class 7. Say: **Think of the table setting as a puzzle with all the pieces fitting together attractively.**

TEACHING MATERIALS

Courtesy Begins at Home - Class 1

- ❏ "Entry Display" - poster & place setting (See "Entry Display," page 10.)
- ❏ one workbook per student (Provide appropriate number of workbooks and place on each team's table.)
- ❏ one folder per student (See explanation of Copy Sheet # 1, page 106.)
- ❏ one place card per student with his name (See explanation of Copy Sheet # 4, page 107) placed at assigned seating; option: samples of decorative place cards at the team tables
- ❏ one "Pop Quiz" per student (See explanation of Copy Sheet # 3) placed in team folders
- ❏ camera & film for team leaders to photograph each others' teams
- ❏ option: example of a news article about manners (page 23 # 6)
- ❏ four copies of the skit "Meet Oops" (pages 19 & 20)
- ❏ props for skit placed on the table where the action will take place: one real or play telephone, sound of ringing telephone (recording or toy telephone), soup bowl with water, soup spoon, several crackers, drinking straw in paper wrapping, roll of paper towels, & vest for "Oops" to wear
- ❏ "Teaching the Table Setting" - basic place setting: fork, knife, spoon, napkin, plate, & glassware (See "Teaching the Table Setting" on page 10.)
- ❏ snack - pudding or applesauce
- ❏ *For one or a few students, spread three layers of pudding with two layers of whipped cream in between in a parfait glass. Top with dollop of whipped cream & candy sprinkles. Place saucer and paper doily under parfait glass and a tall teaspoon beside it. Say,* **The spoon is returned to the saucer after use.**
- ❏ "Materials for All Classes" (page 9)

Introductions - Class 2

- ❏ "Entry Display" - poster & place setting (See "Entry Display," page 10) Add real or plastic bread, bread and butter plate, & butter spreader to place setting.
- ❏ one photocopy of team picture per student to paste over illustration on "Set for Success" cover sheet (Original photograph is given to team leader at Class 8.)
- ❏ characters' props with name tags or name tags only to practice introducing others (pages 32 - 34) and other lessons in the course (Use Copy Sheet # 9 for name tags.) Suggested props are, Oops - vest, Rose Valentine - silk flower, Heloise Hamilton - clip on earrings, Maddie Oopsman - purse, Mark Oopsman - jacket, The Reverend Divine - Bible, Mrs. Stagemaster - "script," Governor Powers - flag, Dr. Spleen - toy stethoscope, Alexandria Hamilton - blazer or sweater, Paul Lite - wrist band, Mamaw Oopsman - shawl, Coach Freestyle - whistles, Eddie

Kit - warm-up jacket, Joy Givens - scarf, Minnie Frenz - necklace, Rudy Loudman - cap

❑ Parent's Letter (See explanation of Copy Sheet # 7, page 108.)
❑ four copies of the skit "Oops Skips the Introductions," page 29
❑ snack - basket holding a slice of bread or a roll for each person, including the team leader (A slice of French bread may be the easiest to use and the most economical.)
❑ one butter knife and plate holding a pat of butter per person and placed at each team's table
❑ for each person - small plate, knife, napkin, & cup of water or other beverage (Place on teams' tables.)   You may want to use paper and plastic supplies.
❑ "Materials for All Classes" (page 9)

Conversation - Class 3

❑ "Entry Display" - variety of beverage glasses, cups, & pitchers; basket of tea bags
❑ assigned questions for team leaders (Make copies of Q & A, pages 41 - 44. Cut out questions, assign them to team leaders, and place them with team folders.) *When assigning questions to one or a few students, clip a few of the answers to the questions for students to read. Students draw questions from a container.*
❑ index card for each person (page 46) placed in team folder
❑ decorative gift bag with tissue or a wrapped gift for Q & A # 8 (page 43)
❑ unopened carbonated beverage can for demonstration (page 47)
❑ extra news articles to use if needed for teams to practice conversation (page 48)
❑ two copies of the skit "Mini Mint Skit," page 40, & three copies of the skit "Excuse Me" (page 45)
❑ props for skits - vest for Oops to wear
❑ "Teaching the Table Setting" - the basic setting with the coffee cup, saucer, & teaspoon included
❑ Snack - soft drinks with cherries or fruit juice; roll of breath mints per team table
❑ *milk shake or hot chocolate for one or a few students*
❑ "Materials for All Classes" (page 9)

Telephone Etiquette - Class 4

❑ "Entry Display" - telephones, note pad, pencil, telephone directory & address book
❑ note pad supplies on each team's table (Provide the following for each student)
   1. 15 to 20 pieces of note pad size paper. To make your own sheets: fold four 8 1/2" x 11" sheets of paper into quarters & cut along creases
   2. 10" piece of 1/8" width ribbon for each note pad
   3. pattern in same size as note paper with holes punched and centered 1 1/2" apart at the top
   4. *Use a specific shape, for example a heart, for one or a few students.*

❏ recorder and "Hello" recording (page 50) Make a brief recording of a ringing telephone and different people answering in a variety of ways.   A preschool child's answering "Hello" is an entertaining way to conclude the recording.

❏ three copies of the skit "Rose Is Invited" (pages 54 - 55)

❏ props for skit - vest for Oops, two real or play telephones, & sound of a ringing telephone (recording or play telephone)

❏ "Teaching the Table Setting" - the basic setting with the soup bowl, soup spoon, & handful of soup crackers included

❏ snack - for each place: a napkin & a helping of soup crackers, access to drinking water

❏ *soup for one or a few students*

❏ "Materials for All Classes" (page 9)

Guest Relations - Class 5

❏ "Entry Display" - Cake: words on cake are **Oops, It's Your Birthday.**
Serve a white cake, unless you know the preferences of all your students.

❏ cake knife and cake server placed with cake

❏ for each person - small plate, napkin, fork, & cup placed near the cake

❏ a copy of punch recipe at each place (See explanation of Copy Sheet # 9, page 108)

❏ ingredients for punch, can opener & ice, punch bowl & ladle placed by cake

❏ gift bag filled with decorative tissue & helium balloon attached and placed at each team's table. Use team colors. *Tie balloons to the chairs of one or a few students.*

❏ invitations you have received (weddings, graduations, open houses, parties) placed on team tables for students to examine

❏ for "Birthday Party Walk-Through":
1. paper shapes to represent areas: guest room door knob (small circle), party tray (large circle), thermostat (rectangle). *If you teach in a home, one or a few students go to the actual areas.*
2. guest's jacket
3. Optional: a few broken crackers on the "party tray."

❏ greeting card and gift bag as prop to demonstrate how to receive a gift (page 64)

❏ "Teaching the Table Setting" - the basic setting with the salad plate; salad fork & knife; real or plastic lettuce, tomato, and/or cheese included

❏ snack - birthday cake and punch. *Serve cup cakes to one or a few students.*

❏ "Materials for All Classes" (page 9)

Manners Away from Home - Class 6

❏ "Entry Display" - sports equipment, toy cars, figures & pictures of churches

❏ trophy or medal for each team table

❏ nine chairs in three rows of three placed at an angle at the front of the classroom, so that they are not directly facing the teams' tables. (Angle rows so "The

Reverend's" back will not be toward the class during "Attending Church.")
Set-up at least two rows of two chairs for one or a few students.

❑ characters' props & name tags for role playing (pages 71 - 74)
❑ option: record the starting of a car engine for "Riding in a Car" (page 72)
❑ option: hymnal & note pad with pencil under Rudy's chair. See "Preparation" in the lesson plans.
❑ 4 badminton or tennis racquets for "Participating in Sports" (page 74)
❑ masking tape to apply to floor for a tennis "net" & an "elevator" (pages 74 and 75) Allow room for swinging real or imaginary racquets.
❑ small cup of water placed with teaching aids for demonstration (page 75)
❑ copies of parent's letter placed in team folders (See Copy Sheet # 10, page 108)
❑ cloth napkin per student placed on teams' tables for students to practice napkin folding (page 76)
❑ "Teaching the Table Setting" - the basic setting with the soup spoon & teaspoon; salad, dessert & seafood forks; butter knife; bread & butter plate; coffee cup & saucer included
❑ snack - for each place (Examples are, popcorn, chips, peanuts, & pretzels.)
❑ napkins & access to drinking water
❑ "Materials for All Classes," (page 9)

Table Manners - Class 7

❑ "Entry Display" - large gift wrapped box *(gift bag for one or a few students)* & grocery bag to carry food items to a food bank
❑ magazine pictures of 3 dining styles: formal, buffet, & family (page 82) Paste the pictures on card stock and laminate them.
❑ serving silverware to show students (page 83)
❑ copies of "Please don't close the book on manners" (See explanation of Copy Sheet # 12, page 108.)
❑ three copies of the skit "Lunch with Mamaw" (page 79 - 80) & a copy of the narrator's role of the pantomime "Oops at the Table" (page 83)
❑ props for skits: vest for Oops, shawl for Mamaw, play or real telephone, sound of ringing telephone (recording or play telephone), music for pantomime, basic setting for Oops and Mamaw
❑ "Teaching the Table Setting" - basic setting pieces for team to practice together
❑ copies of the basic setting pieces (See explanation of Copy Sheet # 11, page 108.) placed at each team's table
❑ snack - appetizer placed on each team table. Suggestions are,
   1. chips & dip
   2. tortilla chips & salsa
   3. one quarter inch thick slices of cheese cut with bite size cookie cutters. Arrange the cheese on a plate with toothpicks, party crackers, & pepper jelly.
❑ small plate & napkin per person, cellophane to cover appetizer, ice if needed, & access to drinking water
❑ "Materials for All Classes" (page 9)

Thank You; Service; & Night Out - Class 8

❑ "Entry Display" - arranged collection of thank you notes that you have received personally

❑ blank thank you notes (See explanation of Copy Sheet # 14, page 109.) in a basket for each team's table *(Offer one or a few students a selection of purchased thank you notes along with envelopes, stamps, and addresses)*

❑ copy of "Manners Word Search" answers (page 86) placed in each team folder

❑ calculator to tabulate final scores (page 88)

❑ restaurant puzzle (page 89) Paste a large picture of a restaurant from a magazine on cardboard and laminate the picture. Cut the picture into one puzzle piece per team. Write a different topic & number on the back of each piece:
  1. Entering the Restaurant
  2. Ordering
  3. Three Don'ts and a Do
  Attach tape or Velcro on the back of each piece to adhere to a board.

❑ "Just Desserts Cafe" job descriptions (See explanation of Copy Sheet # 15, page 109.)

❑ "Just Desserts Cafe" costumes (old jackets, vests, men's white shirts, aprons, & white dish towels) with the job title attached

❑ poster sign with these words written:

Just Desserts Cafe
"Desserts is our middle name."
Just Opened _____   Please Wait to be Seated.
(day of class)
Just the Dessert of the Day

_____

❑ easel or chair for poster sign (Place sign backwards until the "opening" of the "Just Desserts Cafe.")

❑ certificates (See Copy Sheet # 13, page 109.)

❑ original team photograph framed and gift wrapped for each team leader

❑ "Memory Game" poster & small prizes (pages 90 - 91)

❑ snack - desserts for the "Just Desserts Cafe"

❑ cup, small plate, fork & napkin for each person

❑ knife & pie server to cut and serve desserts

❑ beverages; ice & ice chest, if needed

❑ menus, order forms (See explanation of Copy Sheet # 16, page 109), & a pencil for each order form

❑ "Materials for All Classes" (page 9)

COURTESY BEGINS AT HOME

Class 1 Lesson Plans

Preparation

1. Gather teaching materials (page 11 T.Ed.)
2. Assign each student to a team. Assign each team to a table. Choose a bright color for the team folder. Primary colors work well. Contact team leaders (See explanation of Copy Sheet # 2, page 106 T.Ed.)
3. Prepare for the skit "Meet Oops." *For all skits, one or a few students read the skit, perform with the teacher, or invite others to participate. Alter roles as needed. Mark the roles with a highlighter pen. Option: Film their performance.*

Team Time - The first 20 to 25 minutes

1. As the students enter the classroom, greet them and direct them to their assigned tables. Students locate their place cards and paste them over Oops's place card on their "Set for Success" cover sheets, page 91 in the student workbook. Team leaders welcome students to the team and get acquainted.
2. Team leaders take a photograph of the other leaders with the team members posing by the table setting area or "Entry Display." See explanation in "Team Time," page 27 T.Ed.

Teaching the Table Setting (During "Team Time")

Use the following summary to teach "Getting Down to Basics."
1. **We'll learn the basic table setting today and then learn a little more during each class.**
2. Point out the placement of each piece. **The knife blade points toward the plate with the spoon to the right of it. The tradition of this position is to show friendliness, that you're using the knife to dine with friends instead of using it to attack your enemies.**
3. **If possible, all silverware, glassware, and dinnerware should match and be in good condition. Place the pieces evenly at each place setting. Place each setting evenly with other settings at the table. The pattern on the plate faces the diner.**

Opening Prayer

Give thanks for the sponsors of the course and for the students.

Lesson Introduction - 15 to 25 minutes

Make Class Introductions - Introduce yourself (Hello, I'm M_____.) and ask team leaders and students to introduce themselves. After all the introductions, say you are glad to meet everyone in the class.

Give Opening Statements - The name of this course is *Oops, Your Manners Are Showing.* Just as the title says, your manners are always showing, whether they're good or bad. In this course, we want to help your good manners to show. Exercising good manners will demonstrate confidence, maturity, and intellect.

We also want to have fun. This course is designed as a workshop, and we'll ask for your participation. There's an important rule. Whenever I'm talking or someone I've recognized is talking, everyone else should be listening. You may raise your hand and speak when you're recognized; then we'll all politely listen to you. We're off to a good start, and we'll meet some interesting characters along the way.

How many actually wanted to take this course? Raise your hand if you asked your parents to include you in this course so you could learn about manners. Your team leader will give you 100 points for using good judgment.

If you really didn't want to take this course, raise your hand. Thank you for being honest. My guess is that your parents enrolled you. You receive 100 points for obeying your parents. Is there anyone who doesn't know how you got here? Someone signed you up and you came. Raise your hand. You'll receive 100 points because we're glad you're here and want you to feel welcome. *One or a few students indicate their first impressions of studying about manners.*

Perform the Skit "Meet Oops."
Props: See "Teaching Materials" for Class 1.
Roles: Narrator, Oops, Mom (Maddie Oopsman), and Rose Valentine

Teacher: Please give your attention to our narrator, _____ .

"Meet Oops"

Narrator: Today, we'll watch a performance. In it are some of the characters we'll meet in this course. Please pay very careful attention.

The cast consists of _____, who plays Wilhelminanina (WILL hel MEE na NEE na) Oopsman. She is named after her two grandmothers, Wilhelmina and Nina. She is a child who is neither a brat nor is she malicious. She quite simply has no clue concerning the consideration of others. _____ plays Wilhelminanina's mom, Maddie Oopsman. _____ plays Mrs. Rose Valentine, who has recently moved to the neighborhood.

The setting is the home of Wilhelminanina and her family. Please watch very closely. Thank you.

The telephone rings and Wilhelminanina (Oops) comes stomping into the room to answer it.

Oops: *(Picking up the telephone receiver)* Yeah? . . . Ya mean you're not coming over today? *(She hangs up the telephone without a goodbye.)* Well, I wish she'd make up her mind.

Oops flops down in her chair, crumbles crackers into the soup bowl, wipes her hands with the paper towel, and then tosses the paper towel on the floor.

She hangs over the soup bowl with her arm wrapped around it, spooning toward herself and slurping. Then she picks up a straw and blows the paper off the straw. The paper sails toward the students. She uses the straw to blow bubbles in the soup bowl as she rolls her eyes from side to side.

Mom and Rose Valentine enter and talk as though they are continuing a conversation. They walk toward Oops, who quickly puts down the straw when she sees them and picks up her spoon.

Mom: *(To Rose)* Rose, I'd like you to meet my daughter Wilhelminanina. Her friends call her Oops. *(To Oops)* Oops, this is Mrs. Valentine.

Rose: It's nice to meet you. Your mom has told me you've begun _____ this year. Are you enjoying it?

(Name of school, etc.)

Oops: I dunno.

Mom: *(Looks embarrassed and tries to lead Rose out of the room.)* Rose, would you like a fresh cup of French Viennese coffee?

Rose: Oh how nice, Maddie. Yes, I'd love a cup. *(Rose looks back at Oops.)* Goodbye Oops.

Oops gives a slight wave as Mom and Rose exit the room.

Oops: *(Oops dials the telephone and gets a wrong number. She quickly hangs up without a word. She puts her hand to her mouth.)* Oops . . . wrong number.

The telephone rings and Oops answers.

Oops: Yeah? . . . Who's this? . . . Whad ya want? . . . Oh. Hang on.

Oops becomes distracted and returns to eating, as Mom re-enters.

Mom: Who's on the telephone, Oops?

Oops: *(looks "caught" and puts her hand to her mouth.)* Oops . . . it's for you.

Mom: *(Mom gives Oops a glance and picks up the receiver.)* Hello. Yes, this is Mrs. Oopsman . . . Oh, how interesting.

Mom looks down at Oops; Oops looks up at Mom.

Mom: A manners class on _____.
(name of program or day of the week)
Mom looks away from Oops.

Mom: Sign us up right away. How much? . . . I'll send it in today.

Oops is desperately motioning "No" with her mouth and hands as she tries to get her mother's attention.

Mom: Thank you for thinking of us, M_____. I'll help in the class. Goodbye.
(Name of director)

Mom hangs up the telephone and exits. She gestures "Yes" and motions a desperate prayer of thanks. Oops quickly follows after her.

Oops: Mom wait . . . Mom. I think I can get in the drama class.

Applause.

Narrator: Thank you for your attention. Please get your pencils ready; we're having a "Pop Quiz!" Please jot down as many "oops" or mistakes in manners displayed in the performance as you can remember. Your team leaders will pass out the "Pop Quiz" sheets. After the "Pop Quiz," we'll talk about what Oops can do next time.

Teacher: *(After allowing a few minutes for the "Pop Quiz")* Students, please count your answers and write the number at the top of your sheets. Team leaders, mark the points on the score sheets.

Oops's good manners would have shown if she'd known a few things about being considerate of others. Let's see if we can help Oops's good manners to show.

Lead the Discussion: What Oops Can Do Next Time.
How can Oops enter the room next time? She can . . .

1. Walk through the house without stomping.

How can Oops answer the telephone?

2. Say, "Hello," instead of "Yeah."

What can Oops do if someone cannot accept her invitation?

3. Try to be understanding when someone must decline an invitation.
4. Avoid being critical of someone.

How can Oops act at the table?

5. Sit properly at the table.
6. Stop crumbling crackers into a mess in her soup.
7. Put trash in its place instead of on the floor.
8. Stop hanging over her food, guarding it with her arm.
9. Spoon soup away from herself.
10. Eat without slurping.
11. Stop playing with straws.

What can Oops do when a visitor enters the room for the first time?

12. Show interest in the other person; stop eating or playing.
13. Stand up and be attentive when an introduction is made.
14. Answer questions and make pleasant comments.

What can Oops do when she dials a wrong number?

15. Apologize instead of just hanging up on the person.

What can Oops do when she receives a call for someone?

16. Answer politely without being nosy.
17. Ask the caller to hold please.
18. Deliver the message right away.

Team Leaders Distribute the Students' Workbooks and

folders. **Please write your name on the title page of your workbook. Write your name on the front of your folder and insert the pop quiz. Use the first page of your folder to illustrate a manners related topic *or* to write a story or poem about a manners. For theme ideas, look through your workbook after class.**

You may use markers, paints, a collage, or some other art form on this project. Be creative with your illustration or story. We'll show or read this page at the next class. Option: Students complete this project during class. Provide art materials.

Explain Introductory Pages as the students turn to each page.

1. **Title Page**

2. **Purpose page** - Read: **Oops, your manners are showing! That's right, whether they are good or bad, your manners are always showing. After all, manners are how you say and do everything.**

   Have you ever been in a situation when you did not know what to say or do? You can build your confidence and at the same time cause others to feel more comfortable by practicing good manners.

   Have you always thought that practicing good manners is only for special occasions? Everyday of your life is special, and you will often have the opportunity to make others feel special.

   Certainly everyone should learn to use good manners. Knowing the right thing to say and showing consideration for others can become a natural way of life.

   Make personal comments and tell how using good manners has helped you.

3. **Table of Contents**

4. **Cast of Characters** (page 7) - **We'll meet these characters during the course. Today we met Oops, her mother, and a new neighbor Rose Valentine.**

5. **Earn Points for Your Team: Score Sheets** (in the student folder) - **Your team leader will mark the points you earn on these score sheets. We've planned a party for the last class. The team with more points will be served by the team with fewer points at the "Just Desserts Cafe."** The classroom will be set up as a restaurant.

Indicate How Points Are Earned.

1. **Attend class - 50 points**

2. **Bring your workbook - 50 points. You'll be using your workbook in class.**

3. **Complete homework - 100 points. The assignment for the next class is to design your illustration page.**

4. **Learn the Bible verse for each class - 100 points** (Double points are earned in Class 4 for the longer verse.) *Assist one or a few students in learning each verse by making bookmarks. (Write the verse on a strip of card stock and laminate it.)*

5. **"Good Manners Report Cards" will be explained later.** (See explanation of Copy Sheet # 5, page 107 T.Ed.)

6. **Bring information about manners to class - 50 points for each item of information. Examples are, newspaper and magazine articles, books, and poems.** Show an example. **Paste your article to a sheet of paper with holes for your folder. Show the information to your team leader, who will circle your points. Then place it in this container.** Indicate the container provided.

   We'll share this information during class and return it to you. Summarize the information as time permits at the end of each class or ask the student to tell about the article.

7. **If you are absent from class, you will earn points at the next class by showing the team leader your completed homework and by quoting the verse for the class you missed.**

Ask a Student To Read the Verse on page 10. Option: A student
opens the Bible to read the verse. "Even a child is known by his actions, by whether his conduct is pure and right" (Proverbs 20:11). **Who is giving us this message?** (The Lord) **In another verse, John 13:35, Jesus tells us we're known as His disciples by the love we show others. Everyone is known by his actions.**

Lesson Material - 10 to 20 minutes

   Have you ever stopped to consider ways that you could be more thoughtful at home? Let's look at our first lesson beginning on page 11 in your workbooks to help us think of some ideas. We welcome suggestions from team leaders.

Read the Lesson and Ask for Examples. Write the responses
on the board. Students follow in their workbooks on pages 11 and 12. *One or a few students fill in the examples in their workbooks.*

To encourage more participation, ask students to discuss some topics specifically at each team's table. Students share what they could do for their own families. Afterwards, students or team leaders summarize the discussion for the class.

Through these discussions, help students to understand that they can make a difference in the harmony and happiness of their homes.

1. **Be considerate of others by accepting responsibility for personal grooming. Keep your hands and fingernails clean. Trim your nails evenly. Shampoo your hair; brush your teeth; bathe regularly; and use anti-perspirant, if needed. Wear clothes that are clean and neatly pressed.**

2. **Keep your room clean and neatly organized. Do your chores cheerfully and promptly; follow through with your parents' requests. Help your brothers and sisters with their chores.**

3. **Respect the privacy of others. Knock before entering someone else's room. Do not go through others' belongings or use personal items without asking for permission.**

4. **Be willing to share your time, your abilities, and your belongings.**

5. **Take care of borrowed items and return them promptly. If you have time to borrow them, you have time to return them.**

6. **Accept responsibility for what you use. Clean up after yourself and put trash in its place. If you use the last paper towel, replace the roll. If you take out a board game, put it back in the proper place after you finish playing.**

7. **Consider the needs of others. Offer a kind word, a friendly smile, and a helping hand.**

   Try to surprise your families with special efforts of courtesy and let us know about them at our next class.

   Before discussing the next topic (number eight), ask for a definition of shortcomings. **The word means coming up short on doing things perfectly. Shortcomings are faults, mistakes, or imperfections.**

8. **Overlook the shortcomings of others. Fill in the blank with OVERLOOK.** Read as the students follow along in their workbooks. **Do you know it is bad manners to point out someone else's bad manners? In fact, someone else's bad manners do not excuse yours. You might say, "This is what I learned in manners class," and let your family see you setting the example of good manners.**

   Overlooking the shortcomings of others is especially important to remember as you learn about manners, because you'll begin noticing when others are using proper manners and when they are not.

24 ~ Courtesy Begins at Home ~

Dismissal - 5 to 6 minutes

Students discuss and vote on their team name that refers to manners.

1. Each team leader writes the suggestions on available paper.

2. Students write their team names on their illustration pages.

3. Write the team names on the board and later add them to the Table Labels.

4. **Next class, we'll see what happens when Oops comes to the manners class.**

Team Names:

Teacher's Kudos

Congratulations. You are ready for the first class and probably will surprise the students. You will help them discover that learning manners can be fun. Keep up the good work. "My help comes from the Lord, the Maker of heaven and earth" (Psalm 121:2).

INTRODUCTIONS

Class 2 Lesson Plans

Preparation

1. Gather teaching materials (pages 11 - 12 T.Ed.)
2. Prepare for the skit "Oops Skips the Introductions."
3. Write students' names in the blanks (pages 32 - 34 T.Ed.) to practice introducing others. Repeat examples or create your own if needed to give all students a role. Introductions can be confusing; students need practice.
4. Ask a team leader to leave quietly during class to be introduced upon re-entering. Cue to leave: students write "handshake" (page 31 T.Ed.)

Team Time - The first 15 minutes

1. Students paste photocopies of the team picture over the illustration on the "Set for Success" cover sheet, page 91, in the student workbook.
2. Team leaders circle students' points in the team folder. The verse students will be quoting from Class 1: "Even a child is known by his actions, by whether his conduct is pure and right" (Proverbs 20:11).
3. Students give their folders to their team leaders. The team leader asks the students for permission to show their illustration pages during class.

Teaching the Table Setting - 4 to 6 minutes

Use the summary below to teach "Give Us Our Daily Bread" to the entire class.
1. **Today we'll learn about passing and breaking bread, and then you'll have bread to share with your team.**
2. Draw a simple diagram on the board to show the placement of the bread and butter plate and the butter spreader. See Figure 3a on page 99 T.Ed.
3. **As bread is passed, take the closest bread without searching the basket.**
4. **As butter is passed, take a pat and place it on the side of your bread and butter plate, not directly on your bread. Return the serving silverware.**
5. **Hold the bread a little above your plate as you break off a piece with your hand. Use the spreader to butter the bread. Eat the piece of bread and break off another piece, butter it, and then eat it. Whenever the bread is warm, you**

may butter it all at once, but still break it into smaller pieces to eat it.

6. **The tradition is that the poor would collect the pieces that fell when the bread was broken.**

7. Students pass the plates and properly set their knives.

Opening Prayer

A student at each team's table says the blessing within his team. Students place their napkins in their laps, pass the bread and butter, and eat as the class proceeds.

Review - 5 to 10 minutes

Share the Student's Illustrations. As the team leader gives you each folder, make positive comments about the illustrations, stories, or poems. *One or a few students tell about their illustration pages.* Thank all the students for their excellent projects.

Ask Who Surprised Their Families with special efforts of courtesy. Allow students to answer. Thank each student for showing consideration of others.

Read "Good Manners Report Cards" that have been turned in from other teachers and team leaders. **Your team leader will mark your points. Please paste your cards on "My Good Manners Report Cards," the last page in your workbook** (page 119). See explanation of Copy Sheet # 5, page 107 T.Ed.

We'll send a "Good Manners Report Card" home with you so your families may report when your good manners show at home. Return the cards to class and place them in this container. Indicate container you have provided. **You'll receive a new report card to take home each time you return one to class.**

Lesson Introduction - 10 to 15 minutes

Perform the Skit "Oops Skips the Introductions."
Props: Three workbooks (Each performer holds one.) and a vest for Oops to wear.
Roles: Narrator, Oops, "the student," and "the friend"

"Oops Skips the Introductions"

Narrator: Oops is now attending the manners class in which her mother has enrolled her. We see her in the performance today as she is returning to the class with the other students.

Holding a student workbook, Oops enters, looks around, and walks toward "the student."

Oops: Aren't you on my manners team: The "Power Manners Team?"

"The student" nods.

Oops: Did your mom make you take this class, too?

Student: Yeah, I wanted to take drama, so I told my mom I wanted to learn how to act, and she enrolled me in the manners class.

Oops: Me, too. I'd be good at drama. What's today's lesson about anyway?

Student: *(Looking in workbook)* Uh, "Introductions."

Oops: Oh, I don't know anything about that, so I just never introduce anyone.

Oops and "the student" laugh.

Student: Oh, look *(pointing to "the friend")*. She's on our team, too. She could probably help us get more points for the "Power Manners Team." I wonder what her name is. Do you know her?

Oops: Oh, I know her, but I never found out her name.

"The friend" sees Oops and walks toward her and "the student."

Friend: Hello, Oops. Introduce me to your friend.

Oops: *(With her hand at her mouth, looking "caught")* Oops . . . I think class is about to begin; I don't want to miss today's lesson.

Applause. Oops, "the student," and "the friend" return to their seats.

Teacher: Oops found herself in the embarrassing position of not being able to introduce two people she knew. Has this ever happened to you? Let's talk about what Oops can do next time.

Lead the Discussion: What Oops Can Do Next Time.

1. Oops can introduce herself before beginning the conversation. The person will probably then give her name. It's better to introduce yourself and wait for the other person to do the same, than to ask, "What's your name?" Also, if you think someone has forgotten your name, go ahead and reintroduce yourself.

2. It's better if Oops's friend introduces herself to the student instead of putting Oops on the spot by asking for an introduction.

3. If Oops knows even one name, she can introduce the person whose name she knows, and hopefully the other will introduce herself. Say the name of the person you know if you forget one of the names.

4. Oops can say to the student, "I'm sorry, I didn't introduce myself," and then everyone can exchange names. Remember to introduce yourself.

5. Name tags are helpful; however, the purpose of an introduction is not just to find out a name. The purpose is also to show interest in the other person.

Students Open Their Workbooks to page 14. Choose a student to read the verse. "Do to others as you would have them do to you" (Luke 6:31).

How do you feel when someone notices you or treats you as though you're important? Please look at the cartoon on the next page.

30 ~ Introductions ~

What do you see happening in the cartoon? (No one notices or introduces the boy at the doorway.) **What do you think the boy in the doorway is thinking? You may write your idea in the cartoon bubble.** Allow time for a few responses.

As you think about how the boy is feeling and how you would feel, let's learn a little about introductions, and then we'll practice.

Lesson Material - 20 to 25 minutes

Explain the Importance of Introductions.

When someone arrives at your home, stand and let him know you're glad he could visit. Introduce him to others and include him in the activity or conversation.

When you're out with a friend and you're excited to see another friend, don't forget to introduce your two friends. Introductions are important; otherwise, the person is left standing and feeling very insignificant. He may be feeling that he is not worthy of an introduction. Think about the boy at the doorway in the cartoon.

Most people feel uncomfortable in new experiences, so be sure to include someone who's new in your school, Sunday School class, or neighborhood.

It's more important to make the introduction than it is to make it exactly right. What's more important: making the perfect introduction or being sure to make the introduction? (Make the introduction to include the person.) **Why?** (So he'll feel important instead of ignored.) **Making the correct introduction is easier, though, if you know a few rules. We'll practice these rules today.**

Practice Being Introduced.

First, let's practice what to do when you're introduced. Please turn to page 17, "Being Introduced" and interact with the student across from you as I read:

1. **Stand.**

2. **Look at the person and make eye contact.**

3. **Smile.**

4. **Give a brief, reasonably firm handshake.**

5. **Say, "Hello, _____. It's nice to meet you."**

Please be seated and fill in the blank with - HANDSHAKE. The assigned team leader steps quietly out of the room.

Did you ever wonder why you hold out your hand and shake someone else's hand? The tradition of the open hand for a handshake began in an effort to show there was no weapon in the hand; it's a gesture of friendship. You'll probably shake hands more as you get older, but if someone offers you her hand, accept it.

After the performance today, we talked about how to introduce yourself by saying, "Hello, I'm_____," and we just learned how to be introduced. Now let's practice introducing others.

Signal for the Team Leader to Re-enter. Make a "big production" to demonstrate giving honor to the person and saying her name first in the introduction. **Hello, M_____. We're so glad you're with us today, M_____. How wonderful to see you. It's my great honor, M_____, to introduce the manners students to you. Manners students, this is M_____.** Explain what you are demonstrating. The team leader says hello and returns to the team's table.

Call Students Forward to Practice Introducing Others
as they wear characters' props and name tags to distinguish between the roles. Ask a team leader to assist with the props. Read the rule and then the introduction. Direct attention to the characters whose names you are saying as they repeat the introductions after you. Afterwards, the students return to their seats. *One or a few students fill in the examples on page 18.*

Roles: _____ plays Rose Valentine / _____ plays Oops.

Rule: Use Mr., Mrs., or Ms. for adults unless the adult gives you permission to use his or her first name.

Introduction: *Rose, I'd like you to meet my daughter Wilhelminanina. Her friends call her Oops. Oops, this is Mrs. Valentine.*

Oops: It's nice to meet you, Mrs. Valentine.

Mrs. Valentine: Hello.

Rule: Say the honored person's name first. Practice examples of this rule as indicated in #'s 1 - 5:

1
Roles: _____: Maddie Oopsman / _____ : Mark Oopsman

_____ : Heloise Hamilton

Rule: Say the non-family member's name first.

Introduction: *Mrs. Hamilton, I'd like you to meet my mom and dad. Mom, Dad, this is Alexandria's mother.*

Mom and Dad: It's nice to meet you, Mrs. Hamilton.

Heloise Hamilton: Please call me Heloise. Your daughter Oops is certainly a lovely girl.

2

Roles: _____ : Reverend Divine / _____ : Mrs. Stagemaster.

_____ : Governor Powers / _____ : Dr. Spleen

Rule: **Say the VIP's name first. VIP is an abbreviation for Very Important Person. The term refers to someone in a very important position.**

Introduction: *Reverend, have you met my drama teacher, Mrs. Stagemaster?*
Mrs. Stagemaster, this is The Reverend Divine.

Mrs. Stagemaster: It's nice to meet you, Reverend Divine.

The Reverend Divine: Hello, we hadn't met, but I've heard about the fine work you're doing at the school.

Introduction: *Governor Powers, may I introduce Dr. Spleen? Dr. Spleen, Governor Powers.*

Dr. Spleen: Good evening, Governor.

Governor Powers: It's so good to meet you. Thank you for your support tonight.

Whose name would you say first - the governor's or the President's? (President's)

3

Roles: _____ : Oops / _____ : Alexandria Hamilton

_____ : Mamaw Oopsman

Rule: **Say the older person's name first.**

Introduction: Students turn to page 18 in their workbooks to perform:

Oops: Mamaw, this is my friend, Alexandria Hamilton. Alexandria, I'd like you to meet my Mamaw Oopsman.

Alexandria: Hello, Mrs. Oopsman. It's so nice to meet you.

Mamaw: Thank you dear, and please call me Mamaw. Everyone does.

4

Roles: _____ : Paul Lite

_____ : Alexandria Hamilton

Rule: **Say the lady's name first.**

Introduction: *Alexandria, this is my cousin, Paul Lite. Paul, Alexandria Hamilton.*

Paul: Hello, Alexandria.

Alexandria: Hello.

5

Roles: Fill additional roles with students who have not had a turn.

Examples: _____ : Paul Lite

_____ : Eddie Kit / _____ : Hank Yu

Rule: **If those being introduced are about the same age, say the name of the one who's new in town, who's visiting, or who's standing closest to you. Include everyone's last name in introductions, unless you're introducing a family member with the same last name.**

Paul: Eddie, this is Hank Yu. Hank, Eddie Kit. Eddie's family is visiting our church.

Hank: Hi Eddie. I'm glad to meet you. I think you'll like this church. Come in our class, and I'll introduce the guys to you.

Eddie: Thank you. I'd like to meet your friends.

Practice an introduction. Students turn to page 19 in their workbooks
to perform "The Meeting" below.

_____ : Coach Freestyle / _____ : Oops

_____ : Mark Oopsman / _____ : Maddie Oopsman

Oops: Coach, I'd like to introduce my parents. Mom, Dad, this is my swim team coach, Coach Freestyle.

Coach: *(Extending hand to Mark Oopsman)* It's good to meet you, Mr. and Mrs. Oopsman.

Mark: *(Shaking hands)* I'm glad to meet you, Coach Freestyle. Please call me Mark. Thank you for coaching the team.

Maddie: *(Extends hand and shakes)* Hello, Coach, I'm Maddie. Yes, thank you so much; Oops really enjoys the swim team.

Coach: You're very welcome. *(Looking at Oops)* I'm glad you're with us this year, Oops.

Oops: Oh, thank you, Coach, and I'm glad you got to meet before the meet . . . I mean we met before the meet . . . I mean YOU met before the meet . . . I mean . . . See you at the meet.

After the introduction, help people get to know each other. Talk about what they have in common. Use the rules of introduction as a tool to help build relationships.

Demonstrate Two Introductions. In both cases, you are in a hurry.

In the first case, you keep looking at your watch. In the second case, you are attentive and then you excuse yourself to leave. **The same amount of time is spent in both introductions, but which one do you like better? Why?**

Students turn to the last paragraph on page 20 and fill in the blanks: **It is very important to FOCUS on the person being introduced. Give him your FULL attention. When the person walks away, will he FEEL you were really glad that you met?**

Review Introductions.

We've learned a handful of information. Hold up your hand and use each finger to represent each of the five points.

Number 1: **What have we learned that's most important about introductions?** (to make the introduction)

Number 2: **We learned how to introduce ourselves: What would you say?** (Hello, I'm___.)

Number 3: **When being introduced, stand and say . . .** (Hello, it's nice to meet you and the person's name.)

Number 4: **We've learned to introduce others by saying the _____ person's name first.** (honored person's name. Mamaw, this is Alexandria Hamilton.)

Number 5: **After the introduction, help start a conversation.**

Dismissal - 2 to 3 minutes

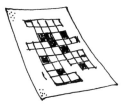

Please read the lesson material in your workbook and work the "Crossword Puzzle" beginning on page 21. Option: Students complete this puzzle during class.

Next class, we'll learn about making good conversation. Please look in the newspaper or in a magazine for an article about something that interests you. You'll use your article to practice conversation with your team. The topic of the article should be appropriate for group discussion. This article doesn't need to be about manners.

Your team leader will give you a reminder letter about the article and about your "Good Manners Report Card." Please show it to your parents.

Please gather your belongings as you leave. We look forward to seeing you at the next class.

Teacher's Kudos

All your preparations and gathering of materials contribute to a smoother class in which the students are able to concentrate on the lesson. Today, your students take a giant step toward considering others, thanks to your help.

# CONVERSATION

Class 3 Lesson Plans

Preparation

1. Gather teaching materials (page 12 T.Ed.)
2. Prepare for the skits "Mini Mint Skit" and "Excuse Me."

Team Time - The first 15 to 20 minutes

Team leaders circle the students' points. Verse from Class 2: "Do to others as you would have them do to you" (Luke 6:31). Students paste news articles on page 34 in their workbooks.

Teaching the Table Setting (During "Team Time")

Use the following summary to teach "Beverages."
1. **The coffee cup, saucer, and spoon are usually brought after the meal. If they are set, however, they are placed to the right of the setting.** See Figure 3b, page 100 T.Ed.
2. Students set the basic setting. They place the coffee cup where the handle may be reached easily by the diner.
3. **Avoid crunching ice, tapping on your glass, stirring loudly, or playing with the straw. Keep your hands in your lap when you are not eating or drinking.**

Opening Prayer

Ask God to guide your conversation.

Review - 5 to 6 minutes

Read aloud "Good Manners Report Cards" and award points. Students open their workbooks to the crossword puzzle beginning on page 21. Read the sentences below as students quickly volunteer answers for the blanks.

DOWN

1. Introduce friends **A S** they enter a party.
2. Mind your **M A N N E R S**.
3. Another word for all right. **O K**
4. **R E** introduce yourself if you think someone may not remember you.
5. Talk about this cable station when you share an interest in sports. **E S P N**
6. **R I S E** when a guest enters your house or room for the first time. (means stand up)
8. Extend this for a shake. **H A N D**
13. Always consider the **O T H E R** person.
14. Abbreviation for Identification. **I D**
16. Say, "It's so **N I C E** to meet you."
17. When you see Coach Freestyle, introduce your parents to **H I M**.
18. "**H O W** do you do?"
19. Introduce men to **W O M E N**.
21. Finish this word: Intro **D U C E D**.
22. Politely introduce one person **T O** another.
23. Except with family members, always include **L A S T** names in introductions. (opposite of first)
26. Two fishermen who meet may talk about a rod and a **R E E L**.
27. **D O N' T** forget to introduce your guests.
29. When meeting Alexandria Hamilton, **S A Y**, "Hello, Alexandria."
30. Stand, look **A T** the person, and give eye contact.
31. Say you are glad you **M E T** the person introduced.

ACROSS

2. It is **M O R E** important to make the introduction than it is to make it exactly right. (opposite of less)
7. Mamaw **S H A K E S** hands with Oops's friends when Oops introduces them to her.
9. A child is introduced to **A N** adult.
10. **A N N O U N C E**. (This is a free answer; just fill it in.)
11. **D E** termine whose name you will say first in an introduction (non-family member, VIP, older person, or woman).
12. Int **R O** duce younger to older.
14. When Alexandria Hamilton's dad introduces himself, he says, "Hello, **I' M** Harold Hamilton."
15. When guests arrive, always **S T A N D** and greet them. (opposite of sit)
19. **W E** help initiate conversation after the introduction. (A word for "us")

20. A **C H I L D** should not use the first name of an adult without permission.
22. Use the rules of introduction as a **T O O L** to help build relationships.
24. Introduce others to government **O R** church officials.
25. You should give this kind of greeting (Opposite of cool). **W A R M**
28. If you **S E E** that someone has not been introduced, introduce her.
29. If a family member's name is not the **S A M E** as yours, include the full name in the introduction. (opposite of different)
32. During our lives we will **O F T E N** need to make introductions. (opposite of seldom)
33. Stand instead of staying **S E A T E D** when you are being introduced.
34. When your name is given **I N** correctly, make the correction.

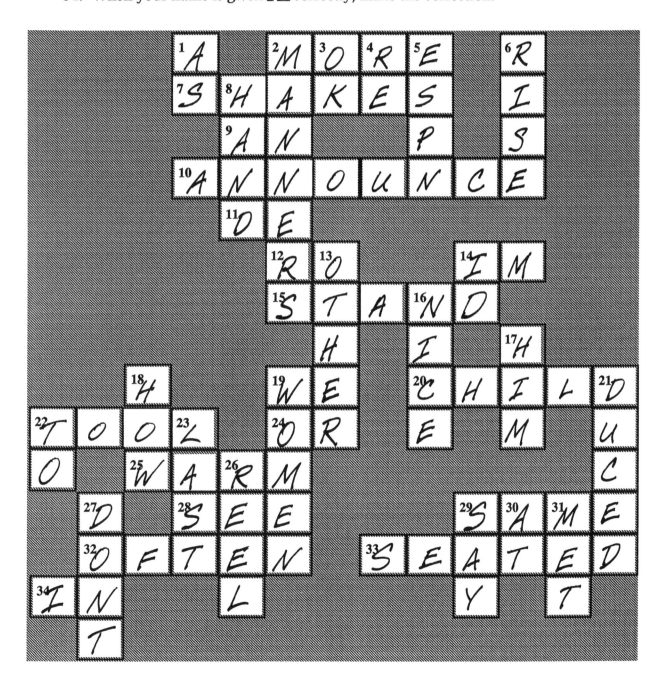

Lesson Introduction - 3 to 5 minutes

A Student Reads the Verse on page 26. "Do not let any unwholesome talk come out of your mouths, but only what is helpful for building others up according to their needs, that it may benefit those who listen" (Ephesians 4:29). **We'll read this important verse again at the end of our lesson today.**

Perform the Skit "Mini Mint Skit."

Props: A roll of breath mints per table.
Roles: Teacher and team leader.   Note: Say breathy "**H**" sounds.

"Mini Mint Skit"

Leader: M_____, I've been wondering if you have a favorite character in this class . . . besides Oops, of course?

Teacher: Yes, I do. I **H**ave two favorites. They are **H**arold and **H**eloise **H**amilton.

Leader: **H**ave a breath mint. *(Leader offers the teacher a roll of breath mints.)*

Teacher: I **H**ave one, thank you. *(Teacher holds up a roll of breath mints and taps it on the leader's roll.)*

Leader: **H**ow about offering some to everyone?

Teacher: I'd be **H**appy to.

Take a roll to each team table, asking a student to offer a mint to the students nearby before taking one himself.

Teacher: People prefer to talk to someone who **H**as used a breath mint when it is necessary and who maintains good dental **H**ygiene.

Lesson Material - 30 to 40 minutes

Introduce Q & A.

Please look at page 27 in your workbooks, as we learn how to enjoy good conversation.

First, it's important to take at least a moment to think before speaking, instead of blurting out your first thought. Don't be afraid you won't have anything to say; just remember to show interest in others.

One of the most attractive traits you can have is caring for others. This trait draws people to you. In fact, if you want to feel less self-conscious in conversation, start thinking about the person with whom you are talking.

Q & A

Team leaders or students read their assigned questions aloud. Give the answers to the questions.

Q. 1: **What makes a good conversation?**

A. 1: **A good conversation is one you enjoy and help others to enjoy as you get to know people. Like the reference verse indicates, do not dwell on negative subjects.**

Q. 2: **Do you mean I shouldn't talk to a friend about something that's bothering me?**

A. 2: **No, you should; it's nice to be able to share your feelings. I mean that you shouldn't continue or allow others to continue in criticism or doom and gloom but help resolve problems in a positive way.**

Q. 3: **Do I have to be a "brain" to make good conversation?**

A. 3: **No, but it helps to be informed about current events. Talk about subjects that are of interest to those in the conversation. Ask polite questions to help learn more about others. Share information about yourself.**

Let's try this. Interact with a team leader or a student.

Teacher: M_____, do you have any brothers or sisters?

Leader: **Yes.**

Teacher: (To class) **Let's try this again.** (To team leader) **M_____, do you have any brothers or sisters?**

Leader: **Yes, I have an older brother and a younger sister. I'm the middle child . . . the well-adjusted one.**

Q. 4: **How much attention should I pay to the conversation?**

A. 4: **Set aside what you're doing, look at the person, and make eye contact. Pay close attention and think about what is being said. Be aware of someone's reactions and respond to them. If someone seems disturbed, ask if he is all right.**

You may be able to make a difference in someone's life because of concern you express toward him. Often you can learn new things by listening to what others have to say.

Also, avoid distracting others with habits such as looking at your watch, yawning, tapping your fingers on the table, stretching, and shaking your leg. A team leader demonstrates the examples of habits and then pretends to realize these habits as they are mentioned. (To team leader) **Do you know what I mean?** Team leader nods. (To class) **Are there other distracting habits you can think of?** (playing with your necklace and hair, biting your nails, and wringing your hands)

Q. 5: **How do I know when I'm talking too much? Sometimes, I get started talking and talking, and I can't stop. I just keep talking, so when should I stop talking?**

A. 5: **Be ready to stop talking if it seems someone has something to say or needs to leave. Consider if there has been balance between your talking and your listening.**

Q. 6: **Are "Please" and "Thank You" really important?**

A. 6: **Yes, definitely. Always include these courtesies to give respect and appreciation. Saying "Please," "Thank you," and "No, thank you," shows that you're not taking the person for granted. The response to "Thank you" is "You're welcome." You may want to add, "I was happy to do it."**

Q. 7: What if someone's opinion is different from mine?

A. 7: Everyone likes to be asked his opinion. Please turn to page 28 #12. Try to see things from the other's point of view. What word do you think goes in the blank? ("I can see YOUR side of that.")

Q. 8: Sometimes, I'm embarrassed when I receive a compliment. What should I say if someone gives me a compliment?

A. 8: It's important to give sincere compliments: to notice the good things that people do, and it's important to appreciate the compliments others take the time to give you.

Let's try this. Interact with a team leader.

Teacher: M_____, I have this gift for you; you're so special. I picked it out just for you and thought you'd like it. Try to give a gift bag to the team leader.

Leader: I don't deserve this, and I can't accept it. Besides, I didn't get anything for you.

Teacher: (To students) I was sincere, and I feel rejected.

Leader: I think I understand. Uh . . . may I have my gift?

Teacher: Yes, of course.

Leader: Thank you.

Teacher: (To students) Just say "Thank you" to a compliment and maybe give a compliment, too, if it's sincere. A sincere compliment is one you really mean. Please look at page 28 #11. It says that sincere compliments are appreciated by almost everyone. Circle the word *sincere*.

Q. 9: Are there certain things to remember about conversation I have in public places?

A. 9: When you're in public with your friends, it's easy to become excited and to roughhouse. Notice the atmosphere around you. Be quiet in movies, theater performances, and restaurants where others are trying to enjoy a night out.

Q. 10: Is there anything I need to remember about greeting people?

A. 10: Remember to greet, that is, to speak to people you encounter. After all, God has placed this person in your life. Say "Hello" or "Good Morning," adding his name if you know it. Speak to people who speak to you. Make sure you're in a safe situation when you greet someone such as when you're with your parents or when you respond to a store clerk.

Stand and speak when someone first comes into your house or room. When a friend approaches as you're talking to someone else, make an introduction and include your friend in the conversation.

Review Q & A.

Write FACTS on the board. **Remember the FACTS about conversation.**

"F" - Discuss FUN topics of interest to everyone.
"A" - Pay ATTENTION to what's being said and to others' opinions.
"C" - Give and accept COMPLIMENTS.
"T" - Say THANK YOU and please.
"S" - SPEAK to people in a friendly way.

Please turn to page 34 in your workbooks and write F A C T S in the blanks. Read: **I remember the FACTS about conversation.**

Introduce the Skit "Excuse Me."

Please turn to page 29, where you'll find some occasions to say, "Excuse me." We'll demonstrate these occasions for you. **Count the number of times "Excuse me" is said in the performance** (8 times). Perform the skit.
Props: A vest for Oops, and any small nearby object
Roles: Oops, Character 1, and Character 2

"Excuse Me"

Character 1 enters the room and begins looking all around for something. Oops enters and stops by Character 1.

Oops: *(Covering her mouth and turning her head to sneeze)* Excuse me.

Char. 1: Bless you.

Oops: Excuse me, I didn't hear.

Char. 1: Bless you.

Oops: Oh, thank you.

Character 2 enters and walks between Character 1 and Oops.

Char. 2: Excuse me for walking between you.

Oops: Excuse me, I didn't hear.

Char. 2: I said, "Excuse me."

Char. 1: Excuse me for interrupting; I see what I'm looking for. Could either of you hand me the _____?
(any small nearby object)

Character 2 or Oops hands the requested item to Character 1.

Char. 1: Thank you. Goodbye.

Character 1 exits. Character 2 and Oops raise their arms to wave goodbye to Character 1 and bump into one another. They raise their hands to their mouths at the same time.

Oops and Char. 2: Oops . . . excuse me.

Character 1 and Oops exit laughing together.

Applause.

Discuss the Skit if time permits.

Look at # 6 (page 29): **Excuse yourself when belching. When someone else belches: what words do you think go in the blanks?** (Just ignore it.)

Students Look at "What not to Say" on page 30.

Just as there are some things you should say, there are also some things that are important not to say. In Matthew 12:36, Jesus tells us we're accountable for our careless words, so choosing the right words is important.

Ask team leaders to pass out an index card to each student. **You'll use your index cards in a few minutes, so be sure to listen carefully. Remember not to say anything that would hurt, offend, or embarrass anyone. If someone has a problem, pray for that person. Ask how you can help. Tell him you're sorry for his difficulties.**

You may see someone on crutches. Resist asking, "What happened to you?" He has probably been asked this question quite a lot. If it's someone you know, express concern by saying, "Oh, you've really been hurt; I'm sorry." This opens the way if someone wants to comment further.

So we don't want to say anything that would hurt, offend, or embarrass anyone. What if someone hurts, offends, or embarrasses you? Be willing to forgive and forget. We all make mistakes and can be insensitive at times. Just as it's attractive to show concern for others, it's unattractive to hold on to hard feelings. It pushes people away from you. Ask God to help you forgive.

Students Write "Oops" on Their Index Cards.

Get ready to hold up your "oops card" if I name something that would hurt, offend, or embarrass someone. For variety, ask different teams to hold up the index cards on different topics.

1. What about gossip?

Students hold up their index cards. **That's right, thank you; you may put your cards down. How could gossip hurt, offend, or embarrass someone?** Students respond. **No matter how so-called interesting the gossip may be, it's just not worth the damage or pain it could cause by your repeating it. Even if no one told you not to repeat it and even if everyone knows it, don't be the one to keep it going. When others want to confide in someone, they'll remember that you don't gossip.**

2. What about not keeping a confidence?

Students hold up index cards and give examples. **Don't repeat confidences** unless someone may be hurt; in which case, tell someone you trust.

If someone continues to ask you personal questions you'd rather not answer, politely say, "I would rather not talk about it if you don't mind." The person should say, "No, of course not" and change the subject.

3. **What about whispering secrets**
in front of others or pointing your finger at others? Would you feel left out if someone pointed at you?

4. **What about telling untruths?**
In conversation, you're not just passing words back and forth; you're building a relationship. A good relationship is based on honesty. Dishonesty breeds distrust.

5. **What about foul language?**
If someone tells an inappropriate joke, simply give a "half smile" to show you caught the joke but didn't think it was really funny. This response is more effective and kinder than rejecting the person. If he doesn't get the point, you may find it necessary to change the subject or leave.

6. **What about bragging?**
Bragging can cause jealousy. It feels and sounds just like what it is . . . bragging. You'll make a negative impression.

7. **What about tattling and teasing?**
Others will appreciate you more if you're sensitive to how they're feeling.

8. **What about contradicting or correcting your parents or**
anyone in public or anywhere? Ask yourself, "Is there a good reason to make this correction?" Give examples of a good reason.

9. **What about complaining**
about chores, food, or not getting your way? Colossians 3:23 tells us that whatever task is before us, we are to do it because we want to please the Lord. Applying this verse to our daily lives will make a difference.

Shake an unopened carbonated beverage can in front of the class. **If I were to pop this top right now after shaking the can, what would happen?** (It would get all over everyone.) **What happens when someone explodes in anger?** (Everyone around is affected.) **Remember this beverage can the next time you start to "explode" in anger.**

Students Discuss News Articles with their teams to practice good conversation. Then team leaders or students report about the experience.

Dismissal - 1 to 2 minutes

Please turn to page 26 in your workbooks and think about what you've learned as we look at the verse again. Read the verse "Do not let any unwholesome talk come out of your mouths, but only what is helpful for building others up according to their needs, that it may benefit those who listen" (Ephesians 4:29).

Please read the lesson and complete the "Conversation Acrostic" on page 35. Option: Students complete this word game during class.

Next Class, we'll meet Rudy Loudman and learn about using the telephone.

Teacher's Kudos

You are teaching a vital lesson. The success of every social, professional, and personal relationship your students will ever have depends on what they learn and put into practice concerning conversation. Be assured, you are making progress.

TELEPHONE ETIQUETTE

Class 4 Lesson Plans

Preparation

1. Gather teaching materials (pages 12 - 13 T.Ed.)
2. Prepare for the skit "Rose Is Invited."
3. Choose a Team Topic on pages 51 - 53 T.Ed. for each team.

Team Time - The first 15 to 25 minutes

Team leaders circle students' points. Verse from Class 3: "Do not let any unwholesome talk come out of your mouths, but only what is helpful for building others up according to their needs, that it may benefit those who listen" (Ephesians 4:29). Students begin eating their soup crackers.

Teaching the Table Setting (During "Team Time")

Use the following summary to teach "Is It Soup Yet?"
1. **The soup bowl is set in front of you on a plate. Place the soup spoon on the plate after use.**
2. **Hold the spoon as you would a pencil and spoon away from yourself.**
3. **Skim the top of the soup so it will cool. Take a drink of water if the soup is too hot.**
4. **Don't put too much soup on your spoon; otherwise, you'll slurp trying to sip it all. Sip from the end or side of the spoon without putting the whole spoon in your mouth unless the spoon is small.**
5. **When there's only a small amount left in the bowl, tip the bowl away from yourself with one hand, as you spoon the soup with the other hand. It's a compliment to the hostess that you want to eat all the soup.**
6. **You may place a few small crackers at a time into your soup.**

Opening Prayer

Thank God that we can reach people all over the world with the telephone and that we don't even need a telephone to reach God. We just call His name and pray. He'll always answer.

Review - 2 to 3 minutes

Read "Good Manners Report Cards." Students open their workbooks to the "Conversation Acrostic," page 35 and quickly volunteer answers.

1. Rise and say "Good**B**ye," as someone leaves your house.
2. It is not polite to whispe**R** secrets in front of others.
3. Interrupt conversation only when nec**E**ssary.
4. **A**sk polite questions to help get to know someone.
5. Everyone is worthy of respec**T**.
6. If a friend approaches when you are conversing, he s**H**ould be included in the conversation.
7. When bumping into someone, say, "Excuse **M**e."
8. Look for opportunities to give sincere compl**I**ments.
9. When sneezing, cover your mouth and tur**N** your head.
10. Don't contradict or correc**T** your parents in public.

A Conversation Enhancer: B R E A T H   M I N T

Lesson Introduction - 1 to 2 minutes

A student reads the verse on page 38. "Call to me and I will answer you and tell you great and unsearchable things you do not know" (Jeremiah 33:3). **J-E-R 33:3 has been called God's telephone number.**

On the next page Rudy Loudman is showing us one way to take a telephone call. Today, we'll learn a better way. First, let's listen to the "Hello" recording. After the recording, we'll ask each team to talk on the telephone. Play the "Hello" recording.

Lesson Material - 30 to 40 minutes.

Place a telephone with each team as the topic is discussed. Read each point under the topic, pausing to allow students on the team to take turns speaking into the receiver as they read the words in quotes. Ask students to follow in their workbooks beginning on page 41. Encourage class discussion.

Team Topic: Answering the Telephone

Sound of a ringing telephone: _____ **Team, please answer the telephone.**

1. Say, "Hello" (not yeah or yo).

2. If the call is not for you, say, "One moment please" or "Just a minute, please." Expressions such as "Hang on" or "Hold on" sound like commands.

3. Immediately notify the recipient of the call. Avoid shouting when you let someone know she has a call. Set the telephone down **GENTLY** and look for the person receiving the call. **Fill in the blank with the word *gently*.**

4. Do not demand to know who is calling or what she wants. Examples - Who is this? Whatchawant? Say: "May I tell my mother who's calling?" Ask this question to inform the person called, not to satisfy your own curiosity. **If you ask who's calling before answering whether or not the person is in, it sounds suspiciously like her "being in" depends on who's calling.**

5. If the caller is a family member or friend, say a few cordial words before handing over the telephone. "How are you feeling today, Mamaw?"

6. Hang up as soon as you hear the recipient speak to the caller from another telephone.

7. Sometimes more than one person will answer the telephone at the same time. Hearing several voices at once is confusing to the caller. Determine who should hang up and who should take the call. It may be better to let the adult or older child in the house take the call. You may want to ask your parents what you should do.

8. If the person called is not available, DO NOT tell the caller that there is no one else at home! (a good safety rule) Say, "He can't come to the telephone right now. May I take a message or ask him to return your call?" **You don't need to tell why the person cannot take the call.** Write down the message right away and deliver it as soon as possible. **Repeat the message and the number to the caller to be sure you have written them correctly. Stick-on notes are sometimes helpful. Ask your family where to leave messages. It's always a good idea to write the name beside every telephone number you write.**

Team Topic: Making the Call

Sound of a ringing telephone: _____ **Team, prepare to make your call.**

1. Think about your call before you dial the number. Have a good idea of what you want to say before you call someone. The person you are calling will not appreciate having to wait while you decide. **Gather information together. Discuss important topics first. Then discuss other topics as time permits.**

2. Do not call before 9:00 a.m. or after 9:00 or 9:30 p.m.

3. Avoid calling others as they are beginning their day. They may be trying to leave for work or getting ready for school.

4. Allow six rings before hanging up.

5. Identify yourself. "This is _____. May I please speak to _____?"

6. If someone you know answers, say a word of greeting especially to parents. "Hello, Mrs. Hamilton. This is Oops; may I speak to Alexandria?"

7. Ask the person you are calling if she is busy. Be sensitive to her situation if you have called at an inconvenient time. She may have company, be involved in a project, or need to leave shortly. "I'm sorry for the interruption; please call me later about our Manner's Class."

8. Be prepared to speak to a recording. If your call is received by an answering machine leave your name, the time of your call, brief information regarding your reason for calling, your telephone number, a thank you, and a goodbye.

9. Apologize for wrong numbers: "Please excuse the interruption." "I'm sorry, I have the wrong number." "I was trying to reach 555-6677." **Avoid asking, "What number is this?" "555" is the number assigned by the telephone company to be used on television, etc.**

10. Avoid picking up the telephone to see if there is a conversation on the line. Check the other telephones in the house before attempting to make your call.

11. Return calls promptly - **that day, if possible.**

12. Ending the telephone call is generally the responsibility of the <u>CALLER</u>. Fill in the blank with the word *caller*. **If there is a disconnection, who should call back?** (The caller should make the first attempt.)

Team Topic: Conversation on the Telephone

Sound of a ringing telephone: _____ **Team, prepare to speak on the telephone.**

1. Speak clearly. The person on the other end cannot see your facial expressions. Your voice alone must convey your words and feelings. **Ask yourself, "How do I sound on the telephone?"**

2. Avoid eating, chewing gum, or making noises with paper, pencils, or other items.

3. Be attentive. Avoid talking to others in the room while you are on the telephone. Excuse yourself if you must talk to someone else. "Excuse me, my mom needs to ask me something." **Say something or make a sound from time to time as you listen, so the speaker knows you are still listening and are interested.**

4. Do not encourage conversation when you have company. "Please excuse me; I have company. May I call you later?"

5. Be aware of your time spent on the telephone. It is important to be considerate of others who need to use the telephone. **Let others know when you plan to spend a long period of time on the telephone or to make many calls.**

6. Always end with "Goodbye."

Allow others privacy when they are on the telephone and avoid interrupting them.

Call Waiting

1. If your conversation is interrupted by call waiting, either disregard the second call or say, "I have another call; could you hold please?"

2. Do not keep anyone holding for long. After taking the second call, say, "I'm sorry; could I call you back? I'm on the other line."

3. When expecting a call, say, "I may need to take another call in a few minutes."

Immediately hang up on an obscene call and tell your parents about the call.

Perform the Skit "Rose Is Invited."

Props: Two tables with a telephone on each, a chair at one of the tables for Rose, the sound of a ringing telephone, and a vest for Oops to wear. Note: Place the telephones where the class can view easily both "Rose" and "Oops" during the performance.

Roles: Narrator, Oops, and Rose Valentine.

"Rose Is Invited"

Narrator: Rose Valentine is about to call her neighbor, Maddie Oopsman. Oops is studying near the telephone. Mrs. Valentine has not talked with Oops since their introduction a few weeks ago. Let's listen to see if Oops has been paying attention in the manners class and learned about telephone etiquette. Will Mrs. Valentine notice a difference?

Rose enters the room, sits by the telephone, and dials. The telephone rings. Oops starts to run into the room to answer the telephone and then slows down as she realizes she should walk.

Oops: *(Politely answering the telephone)* Hello.

Rose: Hello Oops. May I speak to your mother?

Oops: Yes, may I tell her who's calling please?

Rose: Yes, this is Mrs. Valentine.

Oops: Hello, Mrs. Valentine. *(Oops rolls her eyes in thought for a moment.)* Oh, Mom told me your yard was awarded "Yard of the Month." Congratulations, Mrs. Valentine.

Rose: *(Looking surprised at Oops's interest)* Thank you, Oops, and I understand you're taking some special classes. Are you enjoying them?

Oops: Yes, and I especially enjoy a manners class I'm taking. Thank you for your interest. Excuse me, I'll call Mom to the phone. *(Oops looks quite proud of herself.)*

Rose: Thank you. *(Rose looks at the telephone in a shocked manner.)*

Oops gently places the telephone receiver down and exits. She returns after a moment and picks up the telephone receiver.

Oops: Mrs. Valentine, Mom will pick up the other phone in just a moment.

Rose: Thank you, Oops. *(Rose shakes her head in disbelief.)*

Oops waits a moment as she "listens" to hear her mother pick up the other telephone and hangs up right away.

Oops: *(To herself)* I'm gooooood.

Rose: *(Talking to Maddie)* Hello, Maddie. This is Rose . . . I'm fine. I enjoyed talking to Oops just now. She sounded . . . uh . . . different. Yes, I noticed in the community newsletter that she's having a birthday soon . . . . Oh, I'd love to come to her party . . . all right, thank you. Goodbye. *(Rose hangs up the telephone.)* THIS, I've got to see!

Rose exits. Applause.

Dismissal - 8 to 10 minutes

Assign Homework.

We're all invited to celebrate Oops's birthday at our next class. Please read the telephone etiquette lesson and complete the "Polite Scramble" on page 45. Option: Students complete this word game during class.

Students Make Note Pads.

Use the supplies on your table to make attractive telephone note pads for your home. Scratch paper may be used also whenever you make note pads.

Draw a diagram on the board as you explain: **Place a sheet of note paper behind the pattern card and trace the circles. Place two or three sheets behind that sheet and punch holes through the circles. Continue drawing circles and punching holes until all the sheets have holes. Then place all the sheets together. Choose a ribbon and slip one end through one hole and then through the other hole. Tie the ribbon in a bow.**

Assist students as needed; encourage their efforts. Option: Students make note pads during "Team Time."

Teacher's Kudos

What parent would not be happy with you after today? Anyone who calls the homes of your students will be happy with you. And, you are finishing half of the course material. The students are having their eyes opened to a whole new way of looking at their lives, not to mention their silverware.

GUEST RELATIONS

Class 5 Lesson Plans

Preparation

1. Gather teaching materials (page 13 T.Ed.)
2. Write students' names in the blanks for "Birthday Party Walk-Through" (pages 62 - 64 T.Ed.)

Team Time - The first 15 to 25 minutes

Team leaders circle students' points. Verse from Class 4: "Call to me and I will answer you and tell you great and unsearchable things you do not know" (Jeremiah 33:3).

Students paste punch recipe to their workbooks on page 55. Students examine the invitations on the their tables.

Teaching the Table Setting (During "Team Time")

Use the following summary to teach "Salad" and "Napkins."
1. Students set a basic setting and briefly review eating soup properly.
2. Add the salad setting. See Figures 2a and 2b, page 98 T.Ed.
3. **Eat the salad from where it is placed.**
4. **Cut your lettuce a few pieces at a time.**
5. **Wait for the hostess to place the napkin in her lap before you place your napkin in your lap. Loosely lay the napkin to the left of your plate (or to the right if the hostess does) when you're ready to leave. Place it in the center if your plate has been removed. Place the napkin in your chair if you need to leave the table before you're finished eating.**
6. **Fold a large napkin in half, with the fold facing you. Use the napkin to pat your mouth gently. Do not place food from your mouth into your napkin.**

Opening Prayer

Ask God to help you and your students to have homes where He will be served. Offer thanks for the cake and punch.

Review - 1 to 2 minutes

Read "Good Manners Report Cards." Students open their student workbooks to the "Polite Scramble," page 45 and quickly volunteer answers.

Make additional comments:

1. R E S P E C T - Show respect for others wanting to use the telephone.
2. W R I T E - Write the message right away.
3. H A N G U P - Hang up after the recipient of the call answers another phone.
4. P R O M P T - Be prompt about returning telephone calls.
5. P R I V A C Y - Give privacy to the person on the telephone.
6. H E L L O - Answer, "Hello."
7. C L E A R L Y - Speak clearly on the telephone.
8. C A L L - Enjoy making a telephone call.

What you receive when you use good telephone etiquette: a R E T U R N C A L L

Lesson Introduction - 5 minutes

Draw Cake Cutting Diagrams on the board as you explain.

Rectangular cake - Cut along the shorter end and slice the pieces evenly.

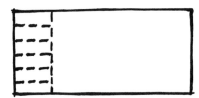

Round Cake or Pie - Cut in half. Cut into quarters and then into eighths. The point of the pie shape faces the diner when the dessert is served.

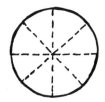

Another way to cut a round cake after cutting it in half is to cut the slices perpendicular to the center line.

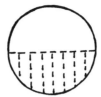

Demonstrate the Use of a Cake Server as you cut the cake in front of the class. Use the knife to cut the cake. Slip the cake server under the slice of cake. Hold the knife parallel to the server using it to balance the slice of cake as you move the slice to a plate. Use the knife to push the cake onto the plate. **Do not use your hand. If you do not have a cake server, use another knife or a fork in its place.**

Serve Cake and Punch with the help of team leaders or students. A handy tip to avoid dripping punch down the side of the cup is to tilt the cup toward the punch ladle when filling. Students begin eating when all the team has been served. Students help themselves to refills of punch during class, if it is convenient.

A Student Reads the Verse on page 48. "Whatever happens, conduct yourselves in a manner worthy of the gospel of Christ" (Philippians 1:27a). **Whatever happens, whether you are a host or a guest; whether you're having fun or not, conduct yourselves in a manner that honors the Lord.**

Lesson Material - 25 to 35 minutes

Today, we'll look at invitations, plan for guests, and walk through a visit. **What kind of party would you like to plan?** Students choose the kind of party.

"Build" an Invitation. **Build along with me on page 55 in your workbooks.** Draw a "house" on the board as you relate the information.

Step 1 - Draw a horizontal line and write "Common" under it. **Call or send invitations to those with a common bond.**

Common

Step 2 - Draw a vertical line on both sides of the bottom horizontal line and write "same" along one vertical line and "day" on the other. **Call or send your invitations to all your guests on the same day, if possible.**

Step 3 - **Invite your guests in plenty of time for them to make plans to attend. "T" is for time.** Make a "T" shape down the middle of the drawing and draw a "door knob."

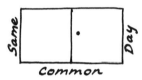

Step 4 - **Take care how you invite someone. Do not put someone on the spot by asking if he has plans; just extend the invitation.** Draw "windows." **Let someone see what you've planned.**

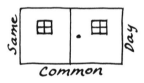

Step 5 - **Top off your invitation with specific information.** Draw the "roof" and write: date, time, place. **Give the day of the week, the exact date, the time, as well as the place, the occasion or type of party, and if it's a surprise. Provide an updated map to your house.**

Step 6 - **Once you've made definite plans with someone, never cancel because you have a "better offer."** Draw a circle around the "house." **If the hostess discovers why you cancelled, she could feel hurt and your reputation could be hurt.** Draw an "X" on the top of the circle. **Don't draw an "X" over your house, and please don't cancel on an invitation unless it is absolutely necessary.**

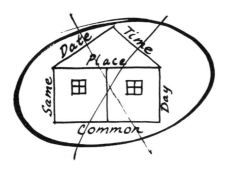

Students Turn to the Invitation Samples on pages 56 and 57 in
their workbooks. **Notice R.S.V.P. Have you ever seen R.S.V.P. on an invitation? R.S.V.P. is an abbreviation for the French words *Respondez, s'il vous plait.* The phrase translates "Respond, please" and means let a host know whether or not you're accepting the invitation.**

Respond as soon as possible. Don't wait more than two or three days to respond. Refer to these samples when you're planning to send invitations.

Teach How to Prepare for Guests. **After making and sending the invitation, it's time to prepare for your guests. Please turn to page 49, "Before the Guests Arrive."**

1. **Make preparations as much in advance as possible for a party so you can focus more attention on your guests. Can you name some ways to prepare ahead for our party** (name of the party the class selected)? Examples in the student workbook are: clean house, rearrange furniture, decorate, set the table, prepare food, make name tags, and get clothes ready.

   Making a check list can be helpful, too. Preparing ahead is a good idea even when you're getting ready for school each day.

2. Students choose a party time and fill in their blanks as you read:
   It's a good idea to be ready for guests at least 30 minutes ahead of time.
   a. **What time is the party scheduled to begin?** _____
   b. **How long does it take you to get dressed?** _____
   c. **Do you have last minute preparations? How long will these take?** _____

d. **Add:**   30 minutes   -   _____
             getting dressed -   _____
             preparations   -   _____
                     Total   _____

e. **Subtract the total of "d" from the time of your party ("a").**
   _____ **is the time to begin getting ready for your guests.**

3. **Let's look at number three** (on page 50), **which poses the question of what to do with your pet when you have a guest. Notice how your guest responds when you offer to take your pet outside during the visit. If your guest does not object, Bow Wow should bow out.**

Students Go on a "Birthday Party Walk-Through."

Now we've extended our invitations and prepared for our guests. We're ready for the visit. Call assigned students forward to play host or hostess and guest for each section of the "Birthday Party Walk-Through." Students go through the motions as you give the information. Involve the rest of the class as the party guests.

First, the Guest Arrives

_____ plays "Host" or "Hostess" / _____ plays "Guest."

The guest comes to the door (classroom door), **knocks, and waits for an answer. When the host answers the door, the guest wishes the host a "Happy Birthday." The host welcomes the guest, takes his jacket or other belongings** ("Guest's" jacket) **to a certain place such as the guest room** (by the paper door knob).

The host introduces the guest ("Host" pretends to introduce "Guest" to the students). **He offers refreshments** (by the paper party tray) **and invites him to have a seat or to participate in the activities. Thank you, gracious host and welcomed guest, you may return to your seats.**

Now, the Guest Visits

_____: "Host" or "Hostess" / _____: "Guest." Ask "Guest" to wait in her seat until you call her forward.

The hostess considers the comfort of all the guests. She checks the temperature (on the paper thermostat) **and the availability of the food.** She sees there are only a few broken crackers on the party tray. She pretends to spread crackers on the tray. **She fills the drinks and spot cleans the area.** "Hostess" pretends to fill the drinks of the other students.

The hostess visits with all her guests. She displays a relaxed mood, remembering she sets the tone for the party. Does this mean she should have fun herself? Yes, and most importantly, the hostess offers hospitality. What is hospitality? (It is the kindness and attention you show your guests that make them feel welcome in your home.) **What is most important for the hostess to offer her guests?** (Hospitality) "Hostess" returns to her seat. Call "Guest" forward.

The guest does her best to have a good time, showing respect for the home and being helpful as needed. "Guest" asks "Hostess," "How can I help?" **She cleans up after herself, and doesn't help herself to the host's personal items.** "Guest" goes to the "guest room" by the paper door knob and pretends to reach for an item but stops. **The guest doesn't answer the door or telephone without permission.**

She places her food on a plate instead of eating directly from the party tray. "Guest" places a cracker from the paper party tray onto a plate and then eats. **We thank our "host" and "guest."**

Then, the Guest Leaves

_____: "Host" or "Hostess" / _____: "Guest."

A guest leaves when it's time for the party to be over, even if he is the first to leave. "Guest" goes to the students to say good-bye. **He thanks the host and his parents and tells them how much he enjoyed the party.** "Guest" thanks "Host." **The guest or host gathers the belongings** (jacket).

The host goes to the door with each guest, thanking him for the gift, for helping him to celebrate, and for the visit. "Guest" and "Host" go to the door. **The guest calls or sends a note the next day to express appreciation and enjoyment of the visit. Thank you, "Host" and "Guest."**

Receiving a Gift

_____: demonstrates receiving a gift. **Please turn to page 51 in your workbooks. Reading number eight near the top of the page will be helpful when you receive a gift. You may feel a little embarrassed to receive gifts, especially at a party, where everyone is watching your reaction as you open each gift.**

Remember that the person whose gift you're unwrapping is waiting to see if you like and appreciate it. Think about how you feel when someone appreciates your gift? Never make light of a gift.

The student demonstrates as you teach the following:

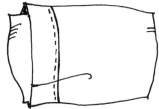

1. **Open the card, read it, and thank the giver.**

2. **Open the gift and thank the giver.** Student looks in the gift bag.

3. **Say something positive about the gift to show your appreciation.**

Students may ask what to say if they really don't like the gift or already have the item. Explain that they would express appreciation for the person's thoughtfulness. (To the student demonstrating) **I'm glad you like the gift. Thank you.**

(To the class) **Let's applaud all the performances today. At Oops's birthday party, Joy Givens gave her a vest. Oops took hers off right away and slipped on the new one. Seeing how much Oops liked her gift gave Joy joy.**

Review the Lesson. **We've talked about some things to consider when extending and receiving invitations, planning parties, and visiting. Entertaining guests in your home as well as visiting others becomes quite natural and enjoyable with practice.**

Anytime you're planning to be a host or a guest, read "Guest Relations" in your workbook. Your guests will feel welcome and you'll be a welcomed guest. Are there any questions?

Ask Who Has Had a Sleep-over and who has gone to one.

Students relate some of their experiences. **Page 54 gives some ideas about spending the night. Join in with the way things are done in the host's home and clean up after yourself.**

While in someone's home, you may hear a family squabble. Just ignore it. What do you do when you hear a family squabble? (Just ignore it.) **Stay out of it. Look at a magazine or watch television.** If a student asks, "What if they want me to take sides?" Suggest this answer for family members, "I'm sure you can work it out."

Number seven suggests gift ideas for a family with whom you are spending the weekend. Read "The Overnight Visitor" on page 51 to prepare for overnight guests. It's fun to help your family prepare for guests.

Show items you've personally prepared for your guests.

Dismissal - 5 to 15 minutes

Please read the lesson and complete "Hosting - Multiple Choice" on pages 58 and 59. Option: Students complete the multiple choice during class.

Next class, we'll take Oops away from home.

Let's play a game at our party today. Play Tic-tac-toe.

Tic-tac-toe

How to Play

Draw the game on the board, and ask each team a question. If the answer is correct, a team member marks an "X" or "O" in a square on the board. If the answer is incorrect, ask the other team for an answer (unless it is a "T" or "F" question). Ask questions until there is a winner. A third team plays the winner.

Questions

1. What should an invitation include? **Answer:** Day, date, time, place, occasion, and if it's a surprise.

2. T or F: Never invite someone over the telephone to a party. **Answer:** False, you may call or send an invitation.

3. T or F: R.S.V.P. is Latin for "Come on in." **Answer:** False, it's French for "Respond, please."

4. T or F: Be sure to ask what your friend is doing on the date of your party so you'll know if he can come. **Answer:** False, just extend the invitation.

5. T or F: Make preparations as much in advance as possible. **Answer:** True.

6. T or F: It's not necessary to be completely ready for your guests at party time; they'll be glad to help. **Answer:** False, try to be ready at least thirty minutes ahead.

7. Within how many days should you respond to an invitation? **Answer:** within two or three days.

8. T or F: Take pets when you visit others, to let them know you feel "at home." **Answer:** False, take pets only with permission.

9. T or F: Divide your time equally among your guests. **Answer:** True, avoid spending too much time with one guest.

10. T or F: It's best to let your guests meet one another and visit on their own while you're serving refreshments. **Answer:** False, introduce them and visit as much as possible.

11. What is most important to offer your guests? H _____.
    Answer: <u>Hospitality</u>

12. T or F: A guest should try his best to have a good time. **Answer:** True.

13. T or F: Planning games or special activities is really a silly thing to do. **Answer:** False, planning ahead isn't silly as long as you're flexible.

14. T or F: If you receive a "better offer" after you've accepted another invitation, you may cancel if you're quiet about it. **Answer:** False, it's unwise to cancel once you've accepted.

15. As a guest, don't answer the _____ or the _____ unless you've been asked to do so. **Answer:** the <u>telephone</u> or the <u>door bell</u>.

16. T or F: Be sure to go through personal items of your host's family to help you know more about them. **Answer:** False, please don't take liberties.

17. T or F: Putting your feet on the furniture helps the host know that you feel comfortable. **Answer:** False, it'll make the host feel uncomfortable.

18. T or F: Politely ask your hostess for shoe polish so that you may shine your shoes after arriving. **Answer:** False, please don't.

19. T or F: When visiting, try to help solve the family's disagreements. **Answer:** False, just ignore them.

20. T or F: If you stay a few days longer than you were invited, the hostess will be pleased she has made you feel welcome. **Answer:** False, she will not be so pleased.

21. Keep your home or party area at a comfortable _____.
    Answer: Temperature.

22. T or F: As your guests are leaving, just make sure they know where the door is.
    Answer: False, go to the door with them and thank them for visiting.

23. For weekend visits, it's thoughtful to take a _____ for the hostess or her family. **Answer:** Gift.

24. T or F: If you keep your things too neat or if you clean up after yourself, the hostess will think you're strange. **Answer:** False, she'll appreciate it.

25. Be sure to _____ the hostess for a good time. **Answer:** Thank.

Teacher's Kudos

You have planned quite a party. Word is getting out about your class. All your preparation has not gone unnoticed. Children are telling their friends about the skits and the food. Parents are appreciative of the positive changes in their children. God bless your efforts.

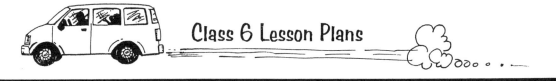

MANNERS AWAY FROM HOME

Class 6 Lesson Plans

Preparation

1. Gather teaching materials (pages 13 - 14 T.Ed.)
2. Review the words to the song, "Take Me Out to the Ball Game" to introduce "Participating in Sports." Plan to call team leaders forward to sing with you. Team leaders will give each other a gentle push when singing the word *out*.
3. Write team's and students' names in the blanks for the "outings" (pages 71 - 74 T.Ed.) Option: Choose a team leader or older student to play Rudy Loudman when "Attending Church" (pages 72 - 73 T.Ed.) Place a book mark in the Bible at Romans 10:9 or a verse of your choice.

Team Time - The first 15 to 25 minutes

Team leaders circle students' points. Verse from Class 5: "Whatever happens, conduct yourselves in a manner worthy of the gospel of Christ" (Philippians 1:27a). Students begin eating their popcorn.

Teaching the Table Setting (During "Team Time")

Teach "A Five Course Meal." See Figures 3a and 3b, pages 99 - 100 T.Ed. After students set the basic setting, ask if they remember the placement of the bread and butter plate and the knife and the placement of the coffee cup. Indicate where to place the silverware for five courses, using the summary below.
1. **Set a seafood fork on the side which provides the most "balance" to the setting. The first course could be shrimp cocktail or maybe escargot (snails).**
2. **If soup is the second course, replace the teaspoon with the soup spoon.**
3. **The dinner knife and fork are for the main course.**
4. **If there are several courses, the salad may be next. Set the salad knife and salad fork closest to the plate. Use your dinner silverware if no salad silverware is set.**

5. When the dessert silverware is set above the plate, the fork is set closest to the plate and comes from the direction of the forks. The spoon is set above the fork and comes from the direction of the spoons. **Remember the FORK is FIRST and the SPOON is SECOND.** If the dessert silverware is not set, it is served with the dessert.

6. To review, remove the silverware and ask the students to set a five course setting.

Opening Prayer

Ask if a student would like to lead in prayer.

Review - 2 to 3 minutes

Read "Good Manners Report Cards." Students turn in their workbooks to "Hosting - Multiple Choice," pages 58 - 59 and quickly volunteer answers.

C   1. Good guest relations should be used
       a. only in your Manners Class.
       b. only at formal dinners.
       c. whether you are the host or the guest.

C   2. Call or send invitations
       a. 10 months to three years ahead.
       b. 10 weeks to three months ahead.
       c. 10 days to three weeks ahead.

A   3. What does R.S.V.P. mean?
       a. Respond please, by letting the hostess know as soon as possible if she should expect you.
       b. Tell everyone else if you will be attending and let it get around to the hostess.
       c. Respond if and when you get around to it.

C   4. When playing party games,
       a. hide in your room unless everyone participates.
       b. call the parents of those who will not participate.
       c. be considerate of those who do not wish to participate.

C   5. What is the MOST important thing you can offer your guests?
       a. Delicious food.
       b. Good prizes.
       c. Hospitality.

A,B   6. As guests leave,
      a. <u>go to the door with each one.</u>
      b. <u>tell each one goodbye.</u>
      c. ask each one how much was spent on your gift.

B   7. If your parents are entertaining guests,
      a. show what you learned in Karate class.
      b. <u>ask your parents where you should be during the party.</u>
      c. go to your bedroom and play your music so loudly that no one will
         forget about you.

A,C   8. During the visit,
      a. <u>respect the home you are visiting.</u>
      b. feel free to use the host's toothpaste, perfume, or any other items
         you want.
      c. <u>clean up after yourself.</u>

C   9. When birthday cake is being cut,
      a. run to the cake and get the first piece.
      b. say, "I'm sorry to be a pig, but may I have another piece?"
      c. <u>wait until you're served or asked to serve yourself.</u>

C   10. When visiting overnight,
      a. tell the family what you do at home, so they may adjust and be
         better hosts.
      b. provide the host with a grocery list of your favorite junk foods.
      c. <u>thank the host for having you.</u>

Lesson Introduction - 1 to 2 minutes

Ask a student to read the verse on page 62 in the workbook. "Show proper respect to everyone: Love the brotherhood of believers, fear God, honor the king" (I Peter 2:17). **You'll meet many people in many situations in your life. It pleases God when your behavior demonstrates proper respect for others. God will honor your deeds.**

Today, we'll practice showing respect for others while "Riding in a Car," "Attending Church," and "Participating in Sports."

Lesson Material - 25 to 35 minutes

Call Each Team Forward to Go on "Outings" and role play
different scenarios. Use the character props and name tags. Team leaders join their teams on "outings." *One or a few students role play in all "outings."*

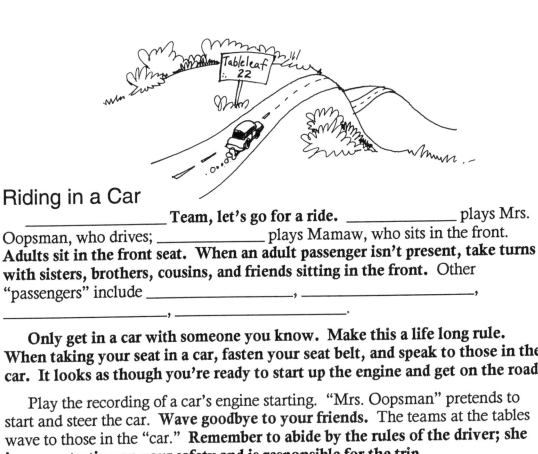

Riding in a Car

_____ **Team, let's go for a ride.** _____ plays Mrs. Oopsman, who drives; _____ plays Mamaw, who sits in the front. **Adults sit in the front seat. When an adult passenger isn't present, take turns with sisters, brothers, cousins, and friends sitting in the front.** Other "passengers" include _____, _____, _____, _____.

Only get in a car with someone you know. Make this a life long rule. When taking your seat in a car, fasten your seat belt, and speak to those in the car. It looks as though you're ready to start up the engine and get on the road.

Play the recording of a car's engine starting. "Mrs. Oopsman" pretends to start and steer the car. **Wave goodbye to your friends.** The teams at the tables wave to those in the "car." **Remember to abide by the rules of the driver; she is concentrating on your safety and is responsible for the trip.**

You're going over a bumpy road now. You're bouncing in the car. **Please don't eat or drink in the car without permission. Make pleasant conversation with those in the car and avoid continuous questions such as, "How many more minutes?"**

Mrs. Oopsman parks the car. Before leaving, gather all your belongings, tell everyone goodbye, and thank the driver. Students say goodbye, thank "Mrs. Oopsman," and return to the team's table.

(To the class) **Please look at page 63, "Riding in a Car" #7: If you travel a long distance, write a _____ you note to the driver or family.** Ask students what would go in the blank. They fill in the blank with - THANK. **When you travel a long distance, write a thank you note to the driver or family and/or the person who invited you.**

Attending Church

The _____ **Team is going to church. The** _____ **Team and the** _____ **Team are in the congregation.** Address the team "at church." **Be on time for your Bible study class and the worship service. Allow time to get your drink of water, use the restroom, and speak to your friends before the service begins.** What do people do when someone leaves his seat during the service and walks down the long aisle to leave? (Everyone turns and watches the person walk all the way out.) **Are people thinking about worship or about the person walking down the long aisle? Read number 1 at the bottom of page 63. Circle the word** *before*.

Now let's attend the worship service. A team leader or older student plays Rudy Loudman. Student roles include _____: Reverend Divine, who stands in front of the rows. In attendance are _____, _____, _____, _____, _____. **A gentleman removes his hat before entering the worship center.** "Rudy" quickly removes his cap, but runs to find a seat. **And gentlemen, allow ladies to enter the pew before you enter.** "Rudy" steps to the side and allows one of the female characters to enter the "pew." **Make room for others coming in.**

When visiting a church, respect the customs of others. Follow their lead unless it conflicts with your beliefs.

Reverend Divine, please ask the congregation to stand and greet one another. This includes students at the tables. Allow a few moments for students to greet.

Reverend Divine, please signal for the congregation to be seated and choose someone to read the Scripture today. A student comes forward and reads the verse: Romans 10:9 ("That if you confess with your mouth, 'Jesus is Lord,' and believe in your heart that God raised him from the dead, you will be saved.") **Thank you for reading from God's Word.**

"Rudy" props his feet on the chair in front of him. **Take care of God's House. Don't use the pew in front of you as a foot rest** ("Rudy" quickly puts his feet down but picks up a hymnal and loudly turns through the pages.) **and be careful with song books and other property.** "Rudy" quickly puts down the hymnal and starts whispering to a student sitting in front of him.

It's distracting to the speaker and to those around you when you talk ("Rudy" stops whispering but writes a note and passes it.) **or pass notes during the service, so listen attentively.** "Rudy" stops passing notes. **Ask yourself, "What does God want to say to me in this service?"** Some people take notes about the sermon. Do any of you take notes? Does it help you to concentrate? **Thank you, _____ Team, for your attention. Gentlemen, if you're sitting by the aisle, please step into the aisle and let the ladies step out.** "Rudy" lets the ladies out. **Thank you, Rudy.**

The team returns to the table. **Please look in workbooks under "attending Church" #7 (page 64). Take an active role as a volunteer in your church. What are some ways you can serve?** (Examples in the student's workbook: Help in the nursery and with summer programs. Help your teacher in class, and clean up areas where you see litter or things out of place.) **What are some other ways to serve?** (Invite friends to church and special activities; pray for your church and its leaders.)

Participating in Sports

Let's "kick off" our sports lesson by standing for the seventh inning stretch. Call several leaders or students forward to sing the song, "Take Me Out to the Ball Game." Students may join in the singing. After the song, thank the students for the inspiration, and address the next team.
_____ **Team, the purpose of sports is to enjoy the game. Give your best effort and help others have fun. We're playing a game in this class with our teams. The more points you earn, the more points your whole team will earn. In physical education classes, remember everyone is there to learn, so take the opportunity to encourage one another.**

Tennis (or badminton), anyone? _____ **Team and** _____
_____ **Team are watching from the "stands."** _____
and _____ play as partners on one side of the "net,"
_____and _____ play on the other side with
real or imaginary racquets. For extra characters, include _____:
Coach Freestyle and _____: Dr. Spleen.

Students pretend to play as the lesson continues. **Remember to be on time for the game; many courts and fields are reserved for a limited period of time. Learn the rules of the game and follow them. No Cheating!**

If someone plays well, say "Good Shot." The audience applauds a "good shot." **If not, say "Good Try." Very often in a game, you'll need to transfer the ball to another player. Roll the ball, hand it to the person, or carefully toss it.** Ask a "player" to choose one of the methods to demonstrate with an imaginary ball.

If someone is hurt, ask if he is all right; offer whatever help you can. Oh, Eddie fell while rushing the net. "Eddie" lies on the floor. **Let's call Dr. Spleen.** "Dr. Spleen" rushes to him. **Eddie is all right and back in the game.**

If you lose, always congratulate the winners. If you win, thank the other team for a great game. Choose a "winning" team and ask that both teams compliment one another's playing. The audience applauds the "players." **Game-Set-Match.** _____ **Team, please go to the showers, I mean, to your table. Good game.**

Please turn to page 64. Let's all read number nine aloud: Good sportsmanship is not determined by whether you win or lose the game. Being a "good sport," however, may determine whether or not you are asked to play again.

Demonstrate As You Explain.

I'll use this chair (Use any available chair.) **to place some leftover popcorn, a crumpled up bag, and a little water. Now, do I have a volunteer to sit in this chair?** Some students may raise their hands. **No one really wants to sit in this mess. You wouldn't want to come into class and find your chairs like this, and others don't want to find what you've left behind.**

Consider those coming after you in whatever you do. Use what you need at the beach, for instance, but clean up after yourself. Using a paper towel, take a moment to wipe out the sink of a public rest room after combing your hair over it. Then wash your hands.

Respect property and the people with whom you share this world. Be observant. Notice the needs of others around you. What can you do if you see someone loaded down with packages trying to open a door? (Open the door.) **Numbers one and two on page 65 suggest ways to help.**

Note the elevator etiquette on number three. Public buildings often have people crowding into elevators and escalators. Take care when entering or exiting. Practice elevator etiquette if a team has not participated or if time permits. **Hold the "open" button if you see someone trying to get on the elevator. When waiting for the elevator, press the button and step aside to allow others room to step out before you enter.**

Dismissal - 5 to 10 minutes

Assign Homework.

Remember to respect people and property whether you're home or away from home. Read the lesson and take the "Away from Home Challenge," page 67. Option: Complete the challenge during class.

Next class, please bring a canned or packaged food from home. We'll use the cans to learn about table manners, and then we'll have the opportunity to donate the cans to a food bank. Ask team leaders to pass out copies of the parent's letter. **Please show this letter to your parents.**

Team Leaders Pass out Cloth Napkins and assist students as they practice napkin folding.

Fancy napkin folding provides another way for the hostess to offer what is most important when having guests. Do you remember what is most important? (Hospitality) **Your napkin folding will pleasantly surprise your family and guests.**

Demonstration 1
1. Open the napkin and lay it flat.
2. With one hand, pick it up from the center, letting the ends fall straight down. With the other hand, turn the open end up.
3. Place the napkin in an empty beverage glass or napkin ring.

Demonstration 2
1. Fold a square napkin in half into a rectangular shape.
2. Beginning at either of the shorter ends, fold the napkin back and forth as an accordion.
3. The napkin opens as a fan when it is placed in a beverage glass. Bend the bottom of the napkin to the side if the fan stands too high.

Demonstration 3
1. Fold a square napkin in half into a triangular shape.
2. Roll the closed side toward the point, just past halfway.
3. Bring the two rolled ends together and place the napkin with the rolls down and the point up.
4. This napkin fold is called "The Sailboat."

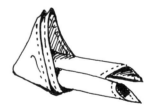

Teacher's Kudos

You're terrific: Now your students know how to act away from home. Their parents will be more comfortable in public settings. Your students' confidence is building.

TABLE MANNERS

Class 7 Lesson Plans

Preparation

1. Gather teaching materials (page 14 T.Ed.)
2. Write these words in a column on the board: Sit, Blessing, Napkin, Eat, Talk, Leave. Write "Hostess" to the left of the column (pages 81 - 82 T.Ed.)
3. Prepare for the skits "Lunch with Mamaw" and "Oops at the Table."

Team Time - The first 15 to 25 minutes

Team leaders circle students' points. Verse from Class 6: "Show proper respect to everyone: Love the brotherhood of believers, fear God, honor the king" (I Peter 2:17). After a blessing at the team's table, students share the appetizer and paste the basic setting pieces to page 108 in their workbooks.

Teaching the Table Setting (During "Team Time")

Teach "Dinner Is Served." Team members set the basic setting and practice together as you instruct them. Use the summary below. Ask the team leader to assist the students.

1. Demonstrate the Continental Style and the American Style of using silverware. See page 100 T.Ed.
2. **Only cut a few pieces at a time.**
3. **Keep your elbows down, raising your arms up instead of out.**
4. **Use silverware from the outside of your plate and move toward your plate with each course.**
5. Show the resting position. See Figure 4, page 101 T.Ed.
6. **Chew with your mouth closed and without unnecessary noises.**
7. **Try to finish about the same time as everyone else.** Show the finished position, Figure 5. **Leave your plate where it is.**
8. **Thank the hostess and offer to clean up. At home, clear your place.**
9. **As a guest, wait for the hostess to let you know when to leave the table. At home, ask to be excused.**

Review - 3 to 4 minutes

    I hope you enjoyed your appetizer today. Your dinner guests will enjoy an appetizer before the meal.

    Read "Good Manners Report Cards." Announce that the next class is the last time to return cards, and ask team leaders to give each student a card to take home.

    Each team chooses a category to volunteer answers in the "Away from Home Challenge," page 67 in the student's workbook.

Riding in a Car
1. Is it a good idea always to grab your favorite seat? **NO.**
2. Should you surprise the driver by bringing plenty of food & drinks to share? **NO.**
3. Is it a good idea to refuse rides from strangers? **YES.**

Attending Church
1. If you use the seat in front of you as a foot rest, will the pastor think you are enjoying the sermon? **NO.**
2. If you offer to help a teacher in class or volunteer in the nursery, will people think you are in the way? **NO.**
3. During a presentation, speech, or worship service, should you and your friends practice the conversation lesson? **NO.**

Playing Sports
1. Should you insist on telling others how to play & showing what they are doing wrong? **NO.**
2. Is skill in throwing the ball the only sign of being a "good sport?" **NO.**
3. Will giving your best efforts add to enjoyment of the game for others? **YES.**

Being Courteous Away from Home
1. Is holding the door for someone just an old tradition? **NO.**
2. Is littering the ground a good way to create jobs for people? **NO.**
3. If you suddenly feel inspired to write a poem or paint a beautiful picture on a public building, does this destroy property? **YES.**

Lesson Introduction - 5 to 10 minutes

Perform the Skit "Lunch with Mamaw."
Roles: Narrator, Oops, and Mamaw
Props: A table with two chairs; a small plate for Mamaw, one for Oops, and an extra one within reach of Mamaw; a telephone; sound of a ringing telephone, a shawl for Mamaw, and a vest for Oops. Action begins with Oops and Mamaw seated at the table.

"Lunch With Mamaw"

Narrator: Today, Mamaw Oopsman and Oops, her beloved granddaughter, have spent the morning shopping in town. They're now having lunch together and are enjoying their special time at Mamaw's farmhouse. Let's see what we can learn about mealtime conversation as we join them.

Oops: Mamaw, I'm having so much fun today. I love visiting you.

Mamaw: I'm glad you could come. I've been wanting to see you too, Dear. *(Mamaw passes a plate to Oops.)* Oh, please have some Brussels sprouts.

Oops: Mamaw, *(Oops starts to refuse but looks at Mamaw and decides to accept politely.)* the Brussels sprouts are soooo colorful!

Mamaw: Thank you, dear. I made them just for you. I'd love to hear about Talent Night. *(Note: say the name of your school program.)* You know your Mamaw was under the weather and couldn't get out in the night air to attend.

Oops: I'm glad you're feeling better now, Mamaw.

Mamaw: Thank you, Dear. Well, tell me about your program.

Oops: There were so many good performances. I'll tell you about one of the funny ones. Maybe it'll cheer you up about missing the show. One of my friends performed a monologue about a girl who would never clean her room. *(Oops looks away as she happily recalls the story.)* She'd bring her snacks into her room, but she'd never take them out. She had a whole family of ants living on one chocolate bar.

Mamaw begins to frown.

Oops: The stinky apples were so old and rotten that the worms couldn't get through them.

Mamaw is wiping her brow.

Oops: And every morning, she'd slide out of bed, because she'd always step down on a slimy banana peel.

Mamaw holds her hand over her mouth as she looks ill.

Oops: The gnats got hung up in the peanut butter . . .

Mamaw is fanning her face.

Oops: . . . that was smeared underneath the . . . *(Oops glances at Mamaw, notices her reaction, and puts her hand to her mouth.)* oops . . . Well . . . uh . . . Dad took the video. We'll just show it to you sometime.

The telephone rings. Oops looks relieved and so does Mamaw.

Mamaw: *(Still looking unsettled)* Would you get that, Dear?

Oops: Oh yes ma'am. *(Oops steps to the nearby telephone and answers.)* Hello . . . Hi Minnie . . . yes, we're finishing lunch. Did Mom tell you I was here? . . . Just a minute please. *(To Mamaw)* Mamaw, may I invite Minnie Frenz for dessert?

Mamaw: *(Regaining her composure)* Why of course, Dear.

Oops: Thank you, Mamaw. Minnie, could your mom bring you out to the farm so you can join us for some of Mamaw's Mississippi Mud Pie? . . . Super, I'll see you soon . . . goodbye. *(Oops hangs up the telephone.)*

Mamaw: I'll cut the pie.

Oops: I'll clear the table.

Applause. Oops picks up the plates. Performers return to their places.

Students Turn to "What Do I Say?" on page 71, number three in
their workbooks. Read or ask a student to read: **Anything that in any way keeps someone from enjoying the meal is OUT OF PLACE at the table.** Students fill in the blanks with - OUT OF PLACE. **When something is out of place, it just doesn't belong. It doesn't fit. It's not in the right place. Anything but pleasant meal time conversation is out of place during dinner.**

Students Read the Verses on page 70 in their workbooks. "Serve
one another in love" (Galatians 5:13b); "[Love] is not rude, it is not self-seeking, it is not easily angered, it keeps no record of wrongs" (I Corinthians 13:5). **Our purpose in teaching good manners isn't to keep a record of who's using the right fork, but we want to help make it easy for you to use the right fork. More important than using the right fork is how you treat people. Giving people respect will honor them.**

80 ~ Table Manners ~

Lesson Material - 25 to 35 minutes

Today we'll practice what goes on at the table. Knowing proper table manners gives you more confidence and enjoyment when dining.

Call Two or Three Students Forward to demonstrate sitting at the table (page 71 in the student's workbook).

1. Let the back of your knees touch the chair.

2. Sit down, keeping your body straight.

3. Slide back carefully in your chair.

4. Keep your legs straight down and still.

5. Be relaxed, but do not lean the chair back.

6. Sit a few inches from the table and slightly lean forward (bending at the waist) as you eat. Do not lean into your plate.

7. Do not rest your elbows on the table as if you are trying to balance your head. Elbows are allowed at the table only between courses and when the meal is finished to aid in listening to conversation.

8. Place your hands in your lap when you are not eating, especially when at a formal dinner.

   Thank the students for their assistance and ask them to return to their seats.

Point to the Words on the Board. All but one of these words depends on the hostess. You will find these words on page 75 in your workbook.
Draw a line from "Hostess" to each word in the column as you say the word (except for the word *Talk*). Ask students to draw along with you in their workbooks.

1. ## Sit
   We've learned how to sit and the hostess will let you know where to sit. Wait for her to sit first.

2. ## Blessing
   Wait for the hostess to ask for the blessing. If she does not, don't say, "At my house, we say the blessing." Quietly say the blessing to yourself.

3. ## Napkin
   Place the napkin in your lap when the hostess does.

4. ## Eating
   Begin eating when the hostess begins or tells you to start without her. The tradition of the hostess' taking the first bite began when she wanted to assure her guests that the food wasn't poisoned.

   In Bible times, the cupbearer would take the first drink to assure that the beverage was safe for the king. Nehemiah, for instance, was a cup bearer.

Fortunately, these days, poisoning by your hostess isn't a great concern, but the tradition of the hostess' taking the first bite has remained.

5. Talk

In earlier days, the hostess would talk to the guest on her right side for half of the meal and then turn and talk to the guest on her left side for the remainder of the meal. All the ladies would turn at the same time. These days, conversation can be more natural, and we don't need to watch the hostess to know to whom we should speak. Do talk, however, with those seated around you.

6. Leave

I won't draw a line to "Talk," but the hostess will let you know when to leave the table by saying something such as "Let's go into the den."

Point to the words on the board again. **The next time you're having a meal, wait for the hostess to do each of these. When you're dining at home, who are your host and hostess?** (Your parents) **Follow the lead of your parents. See if they'll be surprised.**

If you're hosting a friend in your home for a meal, wait until he is finished eating and ready to leave the table before you leave. Your guest will appreciate your consideration.

Show Magazine Pictures of Three Dining Styles.

1. Formal

You are served.

2. Buffet

You go to a table with choices of food. The food might look very good and you might be very hungry, but remember two things.
a. **Be careful about piling food on your plate. It's better to return for more.**
b. **Let older people go first or do what Oops does for Mamaw. Oops offers to prepare a plate for her.**

3. Family

A third dining style is the family style, where food is placed on the table and passed. We'll practice this style today.

Refer to the pictures again for review.

Ask Students To Play the Passing Game on page 73. **Look at the canned foods on your table and choose the one that will be your main course. Pass this one first and then pass the other foods. Pass the foods to the**

right or at least in the same direction. Students pass the cans. **Try some of everything. You may find a new favorite food. Take a medium serving to leave enough for others and to compliment the hostess. Limit the seasoning you add so you won't insult the hostess, suggesting she didn't adequately prepare the food.**

Replace the serving silverware (fork tines down) so that it will not fall from the plate and where the next person may easily reach it. When you pass your own plate for someone to fill it, place your silverware so it will not fall.

Now please set your cans down on the table and choose a food you'd like for a second helping. Can you reach this food without reaching in front of someone else to get it? If not, wait for a break in the conversation and ask the person closest to the food, "_____, would you pass the _____, please?" Then thank the person. Students practice politely asking for their food.

When sauces are passed, pour gravies directly on the food, but place more solid sauces such as jelly on the side of the plate.

Show some of your serving silverware. **If a serving spoon and fork are passed with a serving dish, place the spoon under the food and the serving fork on top (tines down) to remove a helping.** Demonstrate removing a helping.

Perform the Pantomime "Oops at the Table."
See pages 103 - 104 T.Ed. to prepare.
Roles: Narrator and Oops
Props: Table and chair, plate or bowl on the table to define the placement of the action and to hold your notes, music appropriate for a pantomime, a vest for Oops.

Narrator: Due to the night air, Mamaw Oopsman was unable to attend the talent show where Oops and her friends performed. Oops will repeat her performance for Mamaw's benefit.

Oops whispers in the narrator's ear.

Narrator: Oops asks that you follow along in your workbooks as she performs "Oops at the Table," beginning on page 77.

Turn on the music. Oops skips to the table and pantomimes according to pages 103 - 104 T.Ed.

After the Pantomime

Students discuss the "oops" they saw. Ask students to read later all the "oops."

Review the Lesson.

When it's time for your next meal,

1. **go to the table when you're called.**

2. **wait for everyone to arrive and then sit properly at the table.**

3. **wait for your parents to begin eating.**

4. **ask for food to be passed.**

5. **ask to be excused at the end of the meal.**

6. **clear your place and offer to help with clean-up.**

At our next class, tell us about your family's reaction. We're also interested in how you felt about the dining experience.

Dismissal - 2 to 3 minutes

Ask team leaders to pass out copies of "Please don't close the book on manners." **This is an important letter to show your parents. Please read the lesson on "Table Manners" and go on the "Manners Word Search," page 81.** Option: Students complete this word game during class.

Next class, we'll announce the team winners, but everyone will have fun at the "Just Desserts Cafe." Write the dessert choices on the board and ask for a show of hands for the students' preferences. This information will assist you in having the adequate amount.

1.

2.

3.

Please donate your food cans to feed the hungry. Place the cans in the gift box as you leave. We'll gratefully take them to a food bank. God bless you for your contributions.

Teacher's Kudos

Making pleasant mealtime conversation, sitting with feet on the floor, asking for food to be passed, and then asking to be excused . . . . Are you a miracle worker? One more class and the course will conclude. You have worked hard. You are to be commended.

THANK YOU NOTES; AT YOUR SERVICE; & NIGHT OUT

Class 8 Lesson Plans

Preparation

1. Gather teaching materials (page 15 T.Ed.)
2. Write a sample thank you note on the board. Give students an idea of what to say and a specific name of someone to thank: the course sponsor, a church leader, a director, the principal, or a Sunday School teacher.
3. Locate your "kitchen" (serving area); set up the costumes, menus, order forms and cups; place forks and napkins with plates; fill a few plates with desserts.

Team Time - The first 15 to 20 minutes

Team leaders circle students' scores. Bible Verse from Class 7: "Serve one another in love" (Galatians 5:13b); "[Love] is not rude, it is not self-seeking, it is not easily angered, it keeps no record of wrongs" (I Corinthians 13:5). Each student selects a blank thank you note from the basket to write when instructed to do so.

Teaching the Table Setting - 1 to 2 minutes

Use the summary below to teach "Finger Bowls and Dessert" to the entire class.
1. **Today, we'll learn about finger bowls and dessert.**
2. **Has anyone ever been served a finger bowl?** Wait for a response. **Please turn to pages 106 - 107 in your workbooks. These pages will tell you about a finger bowl. If a finger bowl is served, it's usually right before dessert.**
3. **When dessert is served, wait for the hostess to begin eating her dessert before eating your dessert.**
4. **When you're in a restaurant, the good news is you may share desserts. Ask for individual plates and use clean silverware to divide the portion before eating the dessert.**

Opening Prayer

Offer thanks for the food served, for the sponsors of the course, and for the team leaders. Pray that the students will know God personally.

Review - 1 to 3 minutes

Ask who surprised their families at the dinner table after the table manners lesson. Read "Good Manners Report Cards." Applaud all the good manners that have been showing during the course. **People will notice your good manners**.

Ask students to open their workbooks to the "Manners Word Search" on page 81 and volunteer answers. Ask team leaders to refer to their copies of the answers in the team folder to help students find the hidden words.

```
W  A  I  T  L  H  H  B  M  H  G  A  H  T
R  E  M  O  T  B  O  M  T  B  A  B  X  H
Z  Z  Z  B  L  E  S  S  I  N  G  C  X  A
Z  P  R  W  B  B  T  Z  N  S  Z  D  P  N
Z  A  A  L  O  P  E  P  S  P  T  E  L  K
L  B  E  S  A  X  S  Y  A  I  O  Y  G  Z
A  C  A  E  S  I  S  X  B  O  T  G  L  A
P  D  B  T  F  M  Z  T  C  U  X  Z  J  E
P  E  U  P  X  B  K  R  D  L  O  Z  P  E
B  U  F  F  E  T  Z  T  E  P  Z  G  X  U
```

Please **S I T** up straight in your chair and **W A I T** until the **H O S T E S S** asks for the **B L E S S I N G** before placing your napkin in your **L A P** .

T H A N K her for the meal whether it is formal, **B U F F E T** , or family **S T Y L E** where you **P A S S** the food.

Lesson Introduction - 1 to 2 minutes

Ask a student to read the verse on page 88. "Give thanks in all circumstances, for this is God's will for you in Christ Jesus" (I Thessalonians 5:18). **God wants us to go to Him with our needs, but how many times do we forget to stop and thank Him for His answers? Psalm 100:4 says to enter His gates with thanksgiving.**

Everything we have comes from Him, and He is worthy of the time we take to express our appreciation. We're made in His image; we want to be told that we're appreciated . . . that what we do is important. In this same sense, others need to know that what they do for us means something to us.

Lesson Material - 25 to 35 minutes

Ask Who Has Received a Thank You Note. **How did you feel about it?** The students answer. **Let the sender of a thank you note know that you appreciated it. It's nice to keep some of your notes, perhaps in a basket. Notice our display.**

Keep a supply of new notes on hand so you may send them in a timely manner . . . within a week. After we discuss writing thank you notes, you'll have the chance to write one.

Can you think of times, other than when receiving gifts, that a thank you note is appropriate? Look for ideas on the next page (when others have given of themselves through advice, visits, parties, condolences, help with homework or projects, hospitality, or by stepping in during a special time of need). Students name other ideas. **Let's look at what to include in a thank you note. Use the following points as guidelines when writing a thank you note.** Read as students follow in their workbooks or ask students to read:

1. **Start with *Dear.***

2. **Name the gift. Never tell what might be wrong with a gift when you write your note. Do not mention the amount if the gift is money.**

3. **Tell what the gift means to you (where you will wear it, how you will spend the money, how much fun you had, how beneficial the help was).**

4. Tell what the GIVING of the gift means to you. Conclude your note with a parting remark and a closing such as "Love," "Much love," "Fondly," "God Bless You," or "Sincerely." Sign your name beneath the closing.

The next page gives an example of a thank you note, but you'll have the opportunity to write your own today. Call attention to the sample on the board. Encourage students to write additional remarks. Each student should try to complete one well-written thank you note. Some students may ask to write more thank you notes. Writing more depends on the time and notes available.

Tabulate Final Team Scores while the students are writing their
thank you notes. The students turn in the completed notes. Deliver the notes after class.

Please turn to "Oops, You're a Winner," page 91 in your workbooks. Let's read the last statement together: No matter how many points you have earned, the point is that you are always a winner when your good manners are showing. Write the final scores on the board and ask the students to fill in the blank on the page with the final score.

Ask the team members with the fewest points to congratulate the winners. The winners thank them and say they enjoyed the competition. Thank the teams for their interest. Give the "Just Desserts Cafe" job descriptions to the serving team leader for her to consider what jobs the students will perform.

Students Turn to "At Your Service" on page 82.
1. Read this page whenever you plan to help serve food. Today, we'll talk about serving and being served at the "Just Desserts Cafe."

2. Stand to the left of the person as you serve food. Remove food from the right side. Do you remember where your glass is placed in a setting? (Above the knife) Point to where your glass would be set. Pour drinks on the right side, so you won't reach in front of someone. The right side is also the side from which you will remove food.

3. For faster service in a less formal setting, bring two plates at a time and stand between two guests. Don't forget to thank the person serving you.

Study "Night Out."

To feel confident anytime you dine out, read "Night Out" beginning on the next page. We'll put a puzzle together today to help us prepare for the "Just Desserts Cafe." Give a restaurant puzzle piece to each team. Before discussing each topic, ask the student with the next number to read the back of the puzzle piece, and bring it forward to form the puzzle. Option: Complete the puzzle yourself as you give the information for each puzzle piece.

1. ## Puzzle Piece: Entering the Restaurant
   As you enter a restaurant, look for a sign that tells you either to seat yourself or wait to be seated. Follow the *maitre d'*, who leads you to your table and may pull out the ladies' chairs.

2. ## Puzzle Piece: Ordering
   Place your order in a timely manner and say, "May I please have . . . . "
   Thank the waiter or waitress when you're served.

3. ## Puzzle Piece: Three Don'ts and a Do
   Don't play with the silverware or anything else at the table; don't draw undue attention to yourself; don't stack the dishes. Do express appreciation to the person buying the meal.

Encourage Students to continue using their workbooks.

In just a few minutes, we'll visit the "Just Desserts Cafe." I'd like to take a moment to encourage you to review what we have learned in class and read what we have not discussed in class. Please turn to page 92 in your workbooks (page 92 T.Ed.) You'll find the poem, "Oopsdroppers," written by a poet for the students in this course. You will enjoy reading about the Oopsdroppers. Read the poem if time permits.

The next section beginning on page 93, is "Set for Success." Review this information as a reminder of the table settings you've practiced. Please turn to the final part of your workbook beginning on page 109, "Manners to Grow On." This section will prepare you for such activities as looking for a job and attending a wedding.

Open the "Just Desserts Cafe."

1. The serving team leader helps the students choose quickly the restaurant jobs and put on the outfits they will wear. The serving team members wash their hands or use wet tissues and then go to the "kitchen" area.

2. The winning team waits outside the classroom.

3. The "*maitre d'*" turns the "Just Desserts Cafe" poster to the front, shows the "guests" to their seats, and gives a menu to each guest.
   The "Captain" welcomes the "guests" at the table.
   The "beverage steward" takes the drink orders.
   The "server" takes the food orders.
   The "chef" gives the drinks to the "beverage steward" and the desserts to the "server" as ordered.

4. The winning team leader checks to see that the orders received are correct and then dines with the team.

5. The serving team leader assists as needed and then dines after all the "guests" have been served.

Dismissal - 10 to 15 minutes

As the serving team is eating:

1. Thank and applaud the team leaders for their help in the course.

2. Award the gifts and certificates to the team leaders.

3. Award the students' certificates. Students place them in the inside pocket of their workbooks.

4. *One or a few students discuss what they learned in the course.*

5. Play the Memory Game.

Memory Game

How To Prepare

1. Cut 24 pieces of construction paper (31/2"x 4" each) to serve as pockets for 3"x 5" index cards. Paste around the edges of the pockets and attach them in rows on a poster board. Number the pockets and write the numbers on the front of them. See the diagram on the next page.

2. Write half of a phrase on one index card and the remainder of the phrase on another card. See the suggested phrases on the next page.

3. Face the cards backwards in different pockets, scattering the phrases.

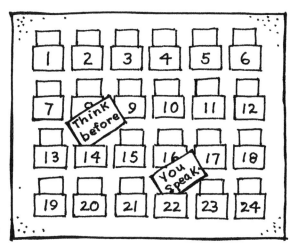

How To Play

1. One student selects a number.

2. Pull the card from the pocket marked with this number, turn it over, read it, and place it face forward in the pocket.

3. The student selects another number. Turn this card, read it, and place it face forward in the pocket.

4. If the cards complete a phrase correctly, remove them. The student chooses a small prize or chooses two more cards. If the cards do not match, turn both cards back over in their pockets. Another student chooses cards. The game continues until all the phrases are matched or as time permits.

Suggested Phrases

1. A rotten apple — stinks.
2. We can use good manners — anytime and anywhere.
3. A dinner knife is placed — to the right of the dinner plate.
4. Think before — you speak.
5. Should I use the seat in front of me — as a foot rest in church?
6. Mom . . . — . . . Telephone.
7. Overlook — other's faults or shortcomings.
8. Speak clearly — on the telephone.
9. In a car, obey — the rules of the driver.
10. Even a child — is known by his actions.
11. Ignore — other families' disagreements.
12. (Names of team leaders or others) — are nice.

Teacher's Kudos

There is a lot of activity for this last class and throughout the course. We hope the course has been enjoyable and meaningful for everyone. We sincerely thank you for teaching it.

You're fighting the good fight. You're finishing your course. You're keeping the faith (II Timothy 4:7).

OOPSDROPPERS
By Kymn

Oopsdropper One
met
Oopsdropper Two
and
found out together
what
Oopsdroppers
do.

They're silly little critters
That you'll hardly ever see – –
If you listen you won't hear them
And they're neither he nor she . . .

Oopsdropper One
and
Oopsdropper Two
picked a likely target
for what
Oopsdroppers
do.

A pretty little girl
Whose manners weren't that great – –
She didn't even remember
To say thank you or sit up straight!

With an
Oopsdropper laugh
and an
Oopsdropper smile
the
Oopsdroppers
dropped
in their usual style.

And this pretty little girl
With a fork in her hand
Quickly fell prey
To their Oopsdropped command.

While trying to remember
The manners she'd ignored
The food on her fork
Flew straight to the floor.

And the pretty little girl
With tears in her eyes
Said, "Oopsdroppers, Mommy,
They oopsdropped, that's why!"

And the
Oopsdroppers
giggled
as Oopsdroppers
do
cause other than children
believers are few.

The mother looked stern
With a mad–mommy face
And the Oopsdroppers
Oopsdropped right on out of that place.

Now don't get feeling gloomy
If clumsy is your name – –
It might be the Oopsdroppers
Playing silly games.

That little girl realized
Soon after they departed
That Oopsdroppers oopsdrop
On poorly–mannered targets.

So . . . always mind your manners
And chances are you'll be protected
Cause those Oopsdroppers oopsdrop
When you very least expect it!

Cast of Characters

Set for Success

Oops at the Table

Copy Sheets

Cast of Characters

(Listed on page 7 in student's workbook)

Oopsman Family

Wilhelminanina (WILL hel MEE na NEE na) Oopsman - Oops
Maddie & Mark Oopsman - Oops's parents
Mamaw (MA'AM maw *or* ma MAW) Nina Oopsman - Oops's grandmother
Paul Lite - Oops's cousin
Bow Wow the Dog

Neighbors

Rose & Moses Valentine

Oops's Friends

Rudy Loudman
Hank Yu
Eddie Kit
Joy Givens
Minnie Frenz

Hamilton Family

Alexandria Hamilton - Oops's friend
Heloise & Harold Hamilton - Alexandria's parents

Professionals

Coach Freestyle
The Reverend Divine
Mrs. Stagemaster
Governor Powers
Dr. Spleen

Set for Success

(pages 93 - 107 in student workbook)

Getting Down to Basics

Dinnerware

Use a matching set of dishes that are in good condition. (Use coordinating dishes if all pieces do not match.) The pattern on each plate should face the diner. Place the setting about an inch from the table's edge. Keep a service plate in place between courses at a formal dinner so that the place is never "empty." Place silverware evenly at each place setting. Place each setting evenly with the other settings at the table.

Silverware

Only set the silverware that will be used during the meal, but always include the dinner fork, dinner knife and spoon for balance. Use the same pattern of silverware, if possible. If not, all forks and knives on the table should match, unless the knives have special handles. All spoons should match other spoons. Silverware brought in with other courses may have a different pattern.

Napkin and Beverage Glass

Place the napkin on the plate, to the left of the fork, above the plate, or in the empty glass. Place the beverage glass on the right above the knife.

Place Card

Use place cards or tell your guests where to sit. Do not set a place card for yourself. Place cards are especially helpful with more than eight guests. Set a place card above the setting, balance it on a napkin, or lean it on the glass if it is not folded.

Figure 1: Basic Setting - Dinner fork, dinner plate with napkin, dinner knife (blade facing in), teaspoon, beverage glass above the knife, place card above the dinner plate

---

Give Us Our Daily Bread

The Bread and Butter Plate

The bread and butter plate separates the bread from the juicy foods on the dinner plate. See Figure 3a on page 99 for placement. Place the bread on the side of the dinner plate if there is no other plate provided. In addition to butter and bread, the bread and butter plate may hold the butter spreader, jelly, spoon for tea or coffee, a tea bag, finger foods or pits. Provide another plate if the meal produces many shells or bones, and place this plate above the bread and butter plate.

Passing the Bread and Butter

As bread is passed, take the piece closest to you. If you touch a piece of bread, you should take it. (Taking a piece you touch is true of any food.) If the loaf is uncut, the host slices or breaks a few pieces and then passes it for guests to slice or break pieces.

If a butter knife is passed with the butter, place it back with the butter after using it. If you accidentally put the butter knife on your plate, return it to the butter tray, if you can do so discreetly. Cut the butter from one end of the stick or tub, and place it on the side of your plate. If a seafood fork is passed with small sections of butter, use it to remove your pat of butter.

Buttering and Breaking the Bread

Put the bread on the plate and butter it there, or hold the bread slightly above the plate to butter it. Do not hold bread in the palm of your hand, on top of the table, or up in the air to butter it.

Break off small sections of bread with your hand (not your knife) and butter with the butter spreader. (Use your dinner knife for buttering bread if a spreader is not provided.) Eat the piece of bread; butter the next piece and eat it. If the bread is served hot, butter all of it at once, but still break it in pieces to eat. This rule of etiquette is derived from the tradition that pieces of bread falling away from the plate or table were for the poor.

Use the dinner knife to butter your vegetables. You may use the butter spreader to butter corn on the cob. Except at the most formal dinners, you may place some bread into the gravy on your plate and eat the bread with your fork.

Beverages

Cold Beverages

The beverage glass is set on the right above the knife. If additional beverage glasses are set, they are placed to the right of this glass. Hold your hand around a lemon or lime when squeezing the juice into the glass. The hostess should remove the seeds before serving the lemon. Avoid tapping on your glass, playing with the straws, or crunching ice.

Hot Beverages

Use a cup and saucer to serve coffee and hot tea. Turn the cup handle where it may be easily reached. See Figure 3b, page 100 for placement. The teaspoon is set on the saucer and returned to the saucer after use.

Place a tea bag in the teapot with hot water until the tea is strong enough, leaving the tag hanging outside the pot. When the tea is ready, use the spoon to press the tea bag against the side of the pot to release the excess liquid from the bag, and then place the bag on the saucer.

Protect the place mat or tablecloth from any used silverware. Place the teaspoon on a paper napkin, or place the bowl of the spoon down on your bread and butter plate or dinner plate.

Napkins or coasters should be accessible when beverages are served. If they are not, be careful where you set your drink. Moisture from the beverage may damage furniture.

Is It Soup Yet?

Soup Bowl

Serve soup in a cup with one or two handles or in a bowl. Hold the cup by the handles if you choose to drink from it after spooning the first sips. Hold the spoon as you would hold a pencil, and skim the top of the soup to give it a chance to cool. Do not try to cool your soup by blowing on it or stirring it.

If the soup in your mouth is too hot, take a drink of water. Do not spit soup out of your mouth. Unless there is danger of severe burning, do not spit any food out of your mouth.

Soup Spoon

Sip from the end or side of the spoon. Do not put the entire spoon in your mouth unless the spoon is small. Do not put too much on your spoon; otherwise, you will slurp in an attempt to sip it all. As with any food, bring the silverware to your mouth and lean only slightly forward. Spoon away from yourself to limit dripping. When there is only a small amount of soup left, tip the bowl away from yourself with one hand, as you spoon the soup with the other hand.

A dinner plate or saucer should be placed under the soup bowl or cup. Place your soup spoon on the plate. If the size or shape of the bowl creates a lack of room on the plate, leave the spoon in your bowl.

Soup Crackers

You may place small crackers or croutons into your soup a few at a time. Crumbling up crackers in your soup looks messy.

Salad

Salad Plate

If the salad plate is on the dinner plate, eat the salad there (Figure 2a, next page). If the salad plate is set to the left of the dinner plate, use the dinner fork to eat the salad there (Figure 2b). If the salad plate is brought in after the main course, it replaces the dinner plate, and the salad should be eaten from where it is placed.

Salad Silverware

Use the salad fork if it is provided. Use the salad knife only if it is needed to cut the lettuce instead of folding the lettuce around the fork. Cutting the lettuce all at once, however, looks messy. Use the dinner knife if no salad knife is set.

Salad Bar

When going to a salad bar, use the spoon or tongs provided. Do not use your fingers. Choose just what you will eat and go back later if necessary.

Figure 2a: Salad served before entree   **Figure 2b: Salad served with entree**

Napkins

The napkin should be in your lap before beginning the meal. If there is a napkin ring, remove it and lay it to the left above the plate. Wait for the hostess to place her napkin in her lap before placing yours. In a formal setting, also wait for the hostess to place the napkin on the table when she finishes. A waiter may place the napkin in your lap.

When placing a large napkin in your lap, fold it in half with the fold facing toward you. If the napkin is small, open it completely.

Use the napkin to: gently pat your mouth as needed.
clean your mouth before drinking.
clean sticky fingers.
dry your hands in your lap after using a finger bowl.
clean the serving silverware if it slips into food.
clean something you spilled.
Do not use your napkin to blow your nose or spit out food.

Keep the napkin in your lap until you are ready to leave the table. Then leave the napkin folded loosely to the left of the plate (or to the right if the hostess does) or in the center if the plate has been removed. Do not put a used napkin on the table during a meal. Place the napkin in your chair if you need to leave the table before you are finished eating.

A Five Course Meal

The First Course

The first course is the appetizer. If a seafood fork is set, you may be served shrimp cocktail, oysters on the half shell, or even snails (called escargot on a menu). The seafood fork is placed on the side that provides the most "balance" to the setting. See 3a (next page) and 3b (page 100). If the seafood fork is set to the right of the spoon, it is either parallel to the spoon (3b) or with the tines resting on the bowl of the spoon.

The Second Course

The soup spoon is for soup that will be served after the appetizer. Sometimes soup is the appetizer. The second course could be either soup or fish. If fish is served, a fish fork and a fish knife may be set (Figure 3b).

The Third Course

The third course is the entree (main course). Use the dinner knife and dinner fork (Figures 3a and 3b).

The Fourth Course

If several courses are served, salad may be served after the main course. The salad knife and fork are for the salad course (Figure 3a). Fruit and cheese may be served after, with, or in place of the salad. Instead of dessert, salad or fruit and cheese may be served. A cheese knife may be set when cheese is served.

The Fifth Course

The fifth course is the dessert. If it is a food that requires a fork and spoon, both will be placed at the top of the setting (Figure 3b) or brought with the dessert when it is served. The dessert silverware is not set in Figure 3a. A long teaspoon (for parfait or iced tea) is placed across the top of the place setting above the dessert spoon and in the same direction. In this case, the dessert fork is placed closest to the left of the plate or brought with the dessert.

Do not place more than three forks, three knives, or three spoons at a place setting. As exceptions to this rule, a seafood fork may be set to the right of the spoons and a dessert fork may be set above the plate.

Figure 3a: Top Row - bread and butter plate with butter spreader, beverage glass

Bottom Row - seafood fork, dinner fork, salad fork, dinner plate with napkin, salad knife, dinner knife, soup spoon

Figure 3b: Top Row - **Salt and pepper shakers, dessert fork and spoon, beverage glass**

Bottom Row - **Napkin, fish fork, dinner fork, dinner plate, dinner knife, fish knife, soup spoon, seafood fork, coffee cup with saucer and teaspoon. Note: The coffee cup and saucer are usually brought at the end of the meal.**

Dinner Is Served

Cutting Food

The American Style and the Continental Style are ways to use silverware during dinner. Choose the most comfortable or the one used by those with whom you often dine.

In both styles, the fork begins in the left hand with the tines facing down into the food. Use the knife in your right hand to cut the food. With the Continental Style, continue holding the knife (or lay it on the top edge of your plate with the blade facing in). Keep the fork in your left hand with the tines still facing down as you eat. With the American Style, after cutting the food place the knife with the blade facing in on the top edge of your plate. Take the fork (tines facing up) in your right hand, and eat the food from it.

Using either the Continental or the American style, cut a few pieces at a time. If the meat is tough, try short cuts back and forth. Do not mix food together into a mess. Keep your elbows down as you cut, raising your arms up instead of out. Except in a formal setting, you may use the tip of your knife or your bread to push food onto your fork.

Silverware During Dinner

Use the silverware farthest from each side of the dinner plate, and move toward the plate with each course. If you accidentally use the wrong silverware, keep using it throughout the course.

Do not motion with your hand while holding silverware. When you stop eating for a few moments or must excuse yourself from the table but will return, place your silverware in the resting position. See Figure 4 below. This placement helps you avoid playing with your setting or with your food. The waiter should not remove your plate when he sees your silverware in this position.

At Meal's End

Chew with your mouth closed and without unnecessary noises. Pace your eating so you finish at about the same time as everyone else. When you finish eating, position your silverware as shown in Figure 5 below. If food remains on your plate, move it aside before properly placing your silverware.

Leave your plate where it is instead of pushing it out of the way and saying you are finished or stuffed and could not eat another bite if someone paid you. In addition, do not stack other dishes on your plate.

Sincerely thank the hostess. Offer to clean up. As a guest, do not leave the table until the hostess starts to leave, saying, "Let's go into the den" or "Shall we go into the living room?" At home, a child asks to be excused; an adult excuses himself. Push your chair in place as you leave.

Figure 4: Resting Position

Figure 5: Finished Position

Finger Bowls and Dessert

Finger Bowls

Finger bowls are not common, however, when used they are served near the end of the meal. The finger bowl (3/4 full of water) in Figure 6a (next page) is shown with a doily, a dessert plate, and silverware. Move the bowl and the doily to the left above the plate after cleaning your fingers. Place the silverware on the table beside the plate (See Figure 6b). If you have a fork but no spoon, place the fork to the right. The dessert silverware is larger than the salad silverware, but the salad silverware is often used.

If a napkin has been placed on top of the bowl, move it to the left beside the bowl. Dip your fingertips into the bowl (one hand at a time), carefully moving them through the water. Use the napkin to dry your fingers, returning it to the top of the bowl. If this napkin is not provided, use the napkin in your lap.

If no silverware is provided, keep the finger bowl in the center; there will be no more courses. If there is silverware but no water in the bowl, keep the bowl where it is; the dessert will be served in the bowl.

Do not use the water in the finger bowl to wipe your mouth. If a lemon is provided, rub it on your fingers.

Dessert

Wait until the hostess begins eating her dessert before starting yours. You may use either the spoon or the fork provided, leaving the other. The spoon is usually used for soft desserts and the fork, for cakes and pies. To use both spoon and fork, use the fork to hold the food in place and the spoon to push or cut the food. A dessert containing fruit, for example, could require both fork and spoon. Coffee may be served during or after dessert.

Sharing Dessert

Ask for an additional plate.

Use clean silverware to divide the food and place half on the additional plate, giving that to the other person.

Figure 6a: Finger bowl served on dessert plate

Figure 6b: Setting after finger bowl has been served

"Oops at the Table"

The Pantomime
(See page 83 in Class 7)

In the Mime
1. Skip to the table and skip away when finished.
2. Face the audience with all actions.
3. Exaggerate your expressions.
4. Make sure the audience understands all movements.
5. Keep the placement of the imaginary props in your mind.
6. Practice in front of someone so you may be cued as to what is especially humorous or what is not clear.

The Performance
The following suggestions start with signal words for each mishap and refer to an imaginary spoon, glass, napkin, food and diner. Enjoy performing this pantomime.

1. Hot Food
Sit at the table and smile. Spoon soup away from yourself and eat. Fan your mouth as though the soup is really hot; take a drink from the glass. Smile in relief.

2. Food Stuck in Your Teeth
With your mouth closed, move your tongue around as though food is stuck in your teeth. Roll your eyes around and grimace. Drink water and smile when the food is dislodged.

3. Full Mouth
Chew with a full mouth. React as though another diner has asked you a question. Continue chewing. Point to your mouth and smile. Pretend to swallow; nod your head and move your mouth as though answering *yes*.

4. Spill on the Table
Reach for your glass and then act quickly as though you have spilled your drink. With your eyes and mouth wide open, throw your hand over your mouth as though you are shocked. Reach for the napkin in your lap to wipe the spill. Very carefully pick up the glass and return the napkin to your lap.

5. Spill on Another Diner
Smile and reach for your glass. Pretend to spill your drink on another diner. Quickly apologize, reach for your napkin, lean over, and attempt to clean the spill from his clothes. Wipe the corners of his mouth. Sit down and smile.

6. ## Spill on Yourself
Reach for the glass and spill the drink on yourself. Look at your clothes and quickly pick up your napkin to clean your clothes. Pull on the garment with both hands and rub the fabric together as though you are hand-washing it. Set your glass upright.

7. ## Drop and Break Glass
Pretend to spill your glass onto the floor. Look down in shock. Look to the diner across from you. Mouth the word *Sorry*. Pull out imaginary money from your pocket and hand it to the diner. Use your napkin to pat your mouth; lay the napkin on the table and skip away.

Oops at the Table
(pages 77 - 79 in the student workbook)

Your food is too hot.
1. Consider that your food may be too hot before eating it.
2. Drink something cold if you have taken a bite of hot food.

A creature or object wants to share your meal.
1. If you notice an unwelcome object on your plate, quietly ask the hostess for a replacement.
2. If the hostess realizes the problem and offers you another dish, accept it.
3. In a restaurant, quietly ask the waiter for a replacement. The other guests should not ask why.

You do not like or cannot eat a certain food.
1. Try a few bites.
2. Eat around the food.

You need to remove something from your mouth.
1. Remove most food items with the tip of your silverware or fingers (however it went in.)
2. Remove small bones or shells with your finger.
3. Remove food that has been chewed with your spoon or fork.
4. Pits may go into your loosely held fist or your spoon.
5. After removing the food item, place it on the side of the dinner plate or bread and butter plate.
6. If it is unsightly, cover it with food on the side of your plate.

Something is stuck in your teeth.
1. Ignore it.
2. Try to work it out with your tongue.

3. Drink water.
4. Excuse yourself from the table and privately remove the item by using a toothpick, dental floss, or by swishing water around in your mouth.

You are asked a question when you have a full mouth.
1. Do not talk with food in your mouth.
2. Avoid putting too much food in your mouth at once. Smaller bites can be swallowed more quickly, allowing you to answer.
3. Continue chewing normally.
4. Smile and point to your mouth.
5. Hope that someone says something to redirect the conversation.

You must take care of something personal.
1. Try to wait until the end of the meal.
2. If it cannot wait, excuse yourself.
3. There is no need to give the reason.

You drop your napkin on the floor.
1. In an informal setting, quietly pick it up.
2. In a formal setting, whether in a restaurant or home, the server may pick it up for you. Quietly pick it up yourself if the server does not.

You drop food on the floor.
1. Leave it until after the meal unless it will damage the flooring.
2. Let the hostess or waiter know if it could cause someone to fall.
3. In most cases, the hostess or waiter will clean the area when guests leave.

You spill food or drink on the table.
1. Remove it with a clean knife or spoon, or dry it with your napkin.
2. Let the hostess know about it if damage will be done.
3. If the hostess is aware of the spill, she will probably clean it.

You spill food or drink on someone.
1. Act quickly.
2. Clean it as well as you can.
3. Have his clothes professionally cleaned, if necessary.
4. Apologize and continue the meal.

You spill food or drink on yourself.
1. Remove the spill with a clean knife or spoon.
2. Use the tip of your napkin to clean the spill.

You break something.
1. Apologize.
2. Buy a replacement or pay for the damage. Repair irreplaceable items.
3. Send a gift and note of regret.

Whatever the "oops," do not continue discussing how badly you feel about it.

Explanation of Copy Sheets

An explanation of each copy sheet is provided on pages 106 - 109. Individual copy sheets are provided in the pages immediately following page 109. Note: Cover the words *Copy Sheet #_* before making copies.

Class 1

Copy Sheet # 1 - **Earn Points For Your Team: Score Sheets**

If your course is taught in more or less than eight classes, reconstruct the score sheets and fill in the dates.

Provide a folder with brads in the team color for each **student** on the team. Insert a blank sheet of paper for the student to illustrate or write about a manners related topic. (See explanation in first topic, page 22.) Make copies of one set of score sheets per student on the team. Punch holes and insert in each **student folder**.

Provide a folder with pockets and brads in the team color for each **team**. Make copies of one set of score sheets per student on the team to insert in the **team folder**. Team leaders circle points on these score sheets for students during "Team Time." Tabulate the scores after each class. Post the scores before each class and place the team folder at the team's table. Students may want to keep scores in their own folders by circling the points they have earned.

Make copies of one set of score sheets per team leader. Attach the set to "Guidelines for Team Leaders," Copy Sheet # 2, so team leaders may understand the scoring before the course begins.

Copy Sheet # 2 - **Guidelines for Team Leaders**

Make a copy of the guidelines for each team leader and attach a set of score sheets (Copy Sheet # 1) to the guidelines, so that the team leader may understand the scoring. Contact the team leaders and give them the guidelines and score sheets before the course begins. Make an additional copy of the guidelines to include in each team folder.

Copy Sheet # 3 - **Pop Quiz**

Make a copy of the pop quiz for each student and punch holes for the student folder. Place the quizzes in the team folders.

Copy Sheet # 4 - Place Cards

Make copies of the place cards on white card stock. Cut and fold the place cards lengthwise. Write the name of each student expected in the course on a place card. Set the place cards at assigned seats. Students paste their place cards over Oops's place card on their "Set for Success" cover sheets, page 91 in the student workbook, during "Team Time" of Class 1.

Copy Sheet # 5 - Good Manners Report Cards

How To Prepare
Make copies on pale yellow or other colored paper; cut apart.

Where To Use
1. Place several in the pocket of each team folder.
2. Attach several to "Teacher's Letter," Copy Sheet # 6.
3. Attach one to each "Parent's Letter," Copy Sheet # 7.

Who Completes
Parents, team leaders, and teachers in other classes attended by your students fill out the report cards. *Sunday School teachers, family members, and family friends may complete the cards for one or a few students.*

How To Process
When "Good Manners Report Cards" are returned to class, read them aloud and give them to the students to paste on "My Good Manners Report Cards," the last page provided in the student's workbook. Four report cards will fill each side of this page. Read each report card aloud in class. Team leaders circle 50 points on the score sheets for each report card as it is read aloud. Team leaders give a replacement report card for each completed one that the students return.

How To Use
Use "Good Manners Report Cards" to reinforce the lessons and help students understand the effect their behavior has on others. If a parent reports that the student says "Please" and "Thank you" at home, say "Thank you for showing appreciation and respect for your family." Specific compliments are better than general ones.

Copy Sheet # 6 - Teacher's Letter

List on this letter the names of students who are enrolled in another teacher's class as well as in your manners class. Attach a "Good Manners Report Card" (Copy Sheet # 5) on the letter for each student listed.

Give the letters to the teachers of these other classes before the beginning of your course. Students respond well to positive reports from their teachers, but consider that some teachers may not have time to participate.

Class 2

Copy Sheet # 7 - **Letter: Report Cards and News Article**

Fill in the date of the next class and make a copy of the letter for each student to take home. Attach a "Good Manners Report Card," Copy Sheet # 5. Place letters in team folders.

Copy Sheet # 8 - **Characters in the Course**

Make copies of the characters' names when needed for name tags.

Class 5

Copy Sheet # 9 - **Punch Recipe**

Make copies of the recipe on colored paper, cut apart, and place at each student's place before class. During "Team Time," students paste the recipes on page 55 in their workbooks.

Class 6

Copy Sheet # 10 - **Letter: Canned Food.**

Fill in the date of the next class. These are duplicate letters; make half the number of copies you need and cut them apart. Place the letters in the team folder.

Class 7

Copy Sheet # 11 - **Pieces for a Basic Setting**

🗐 Make copies of this sheet on cream colored paper. Cut the pieces or give them to students to cut apart.

🗐 Students correctly place the pieces to form the basic setting and paste on page 106 in their workbooks.

Copy Sheet # 12 - **Letter: Please don't close the book**

Sign your name to this final letter to parents. Make a copy of the letter for each student, and place the letter in the team folder.

Class 8

Copy Sheet # 13 - **Certificates**

Fill in the date and signature(s) on the certificates. Make a copy on card stock in the team color for each student and team leader. Fill in the names. Pass out the certificates in class. Option: punch holes for the student folder.

Copy Sheet # 14 - **Thank You Notes**

Make copies on card stock in a variety of colors. Cut, fold, and place the notes in a basket on each team's table. During "Team Time," each student selects a blank thank you note to write when instructed to do so. Provide an ample supply of notes.

Copy Sheet # 15 - **Job Descriptions**

Make a copy of the job description sheet, cut apart each job description, and give the descriptions to the team leader of the serving team when the final scores are announced. The team leader helps the students to choose and fill the jobs.

Copy Sheet # 16 - **Sample Menu and Order Form**

▤ List your desserts, if different from this sample; make copies of the menus on colored paper, laminate, and cut them apart. The "*maitre d'*" gives a menu to each "guest" after seating. The "server" takes the menus with the orders.

▤ Order forms should correspond with the menus. Provide pencils for the "waiter" or "waitress" and "beverage steward."

Earn Points for Your Team
Score Sheets

Possible Points
(Circle points earned.)

Class 1 - COURTESY BEGINS AT HOME _____
(Date)

I (did/did not) want to take this class. 100
(circle one)

Pop Quiz (5 points per answer) .... ____

Total Points _____

Class 2 - INTRODUCTIONS _____

I came back to class. 50
I brought my workbook. 50
I designed my illustration page. 100
I memorized Proverbs 20:11. 100
Good Manners Report Cards 50 50 50
Extra credit information about manners 50 50 50
(newspaper clippings, poem, book)

Total Points _____

Class 3 - CONVERSATION _____

I 'm back again! 50
I brought my workbook. 50
I completed my crossword puzzle. 100
I brought a news article for conversation. 100
I memorized Luke 6:31. 100
Good Manners Report Cards 50 50 50
Extra credit information about manners 50 50 50

Total Points _____

Class 4 - TELEPHONE ETIQUETTE _____

Hello, I'm here today.	50
I have my workbook	50
The acrostic was pretty easy!	100
I memorized Ephesians 4:29.	200
Good Manners Report Cards 50 50 50	
Extra credit information about manners 50 50 50	

Total Points _____

Class 5 - GUEST RELATIONS _____

It's good to see you today!	50
I brought my workbook.	50
The "Polite Scramble" was fun to do.	100
I memorized Jeremiah 33:3.	100
Good Manners Report Cards 50 50 50	
Extra credit information about manners. 50 50 50	

Total Points _____

Class 6 - MANNERS AWAY FROM HOME _____

I came to see new friends in this class!	50
I have my workbook.	50
I completed the multiple choice activity.	100
I memorized Philippians 1:27.	100
Good Manners Report Cards 50 50 50	
Extra credit information about manners. 50 50 50	

Total Points _____

Class 7 - TABLE MANNERS _____

I've been looking forward to seeing you. 50
I have my workbook. 50
I took the "Away from Home Challenge." 100
I brought food for the hungry. 100
I memorized I Peter 2:17. 100
Good Manners Report Cards 50 50 50
Extra credit information about manners 50 50 50

Total Points _____

Class 8 - THANK YOU NOTES & NIGHT OUT_____

Thank you for having me. 50
I have my workbook. 50
I went on the "Manners Word Search." 100
I memorized Galatians 5:13. 100
I memorized I Corinthians 13:5. 100
Good Manners Report Cards 50 50 50
Extra credit information about manners 50 50 50

Total Points _____

Guidelines for Team Leaders

Assist the students in class as needed. Encourage students' participation. Remind them to prepare for the next class. Inform the teacher of special needs.

Assist the teacher in class as needed, for example, by serving refreshments and performing in skits.

Circle 50 points for each "Good Manners Report Card" that the teacher reads aloud in class.

1. Students paste four "Good Manners Report Cards" to each side of "My Good Manners Report Cards," the last pages in the students' workbooks.

2. Give students a report card from your team folder for each one that the student returns to class.

3. Students place the completed report cards in a designated container.

4. Complete "Good Manners Report Cards" for students who exhibit good manners. Please complete at least one for each student on your team during the course.

Lead "Team Time" in the beginning of each class as students arrive at your table. Circle students' points on the score sheets in your team folder (See the attached sample). Assist in activities for each class as listed below.

Class 1 Team Time:

1. The teacher stands at the classroom door with the class roll to greet students and direct them to their assigned teams' tables. Students locate their place cards and paste them over Oops's place card on the "Set for Success" cover sheet, page 91 in their workbooks.
2. Welcome students to the team and get acquainted. Students examine samples of decorative place cards on your team's table.
3. Teams go to "Teaching the Table Setting" Table in their assigned order.
4. Take photographs of other teams posing by the Entry Display or "Teaching the Table Setting" Table.

Class 2 Team Time:

1. Students paste the photocopy of their team pictures over the illustration on the "Set for Success" cover sheet, page 93 in their workbooks.
2. Verse from Class 1 that students will be quoting: "Even a child is known by his actions, by whether his conduct is pure and right" (Proverbs 20:11).
3. Students give you their folders so that their illustration pages may be shown during class. Ask a student for permission before giving the folder to the teacher to show the illustration page to the class.

Class 3 Team Time:
1. Verse - Class 2: "Do to others as you would have them do to you" (Luke 6:31).
2. Students paste their news articles to page 34 in their workbooks.

Class 4 Team Time:
1. Verse - Class 3: "Do not let any unwholesome talk come out of your mouths, but only what is helpful for building others up according to their needs, that it may benefit those who listen" (Ephesians 4:29).
2. Students may eat their soup crackers as the class proceeds.

Class 5 Team Time:
1. Verse - Class 4: "Call to me and I will answer you and tell you great and unsearchable things you do not know" (Jeremiah 33:3).
2. Students paste the punch recipe to page 55 in their workbooks.
3. Students examine the invitations on the team's table.

Class 6 Team Time:
1. Verse - Class 5: "Whatever happens, conduct yourselves in a manner worthy of the gospel of Christ" (Philippians 1:27a).
2. Students may eat their popcorn as the class proceeds.

Class 7 Team Time:
1. Verse - Class 6: "Show proper respect to everyone: Love the brotherhood of believers, fear God, honor the king" (I Peter 2:17).
2. Ask for the blessing at your table.
3. Students pass the appetizer and eat it.
4. Students paste the basic setting to page 108 in their workbooks. Check the placement of the pieces before the students paste them.

Class 8 Team Time:
1. Verses - Class 7: "Serve one another in love" (Galatians 5:13b); [Love] is not rude, it is not self-seeking, it is not easily angered, it keeps no record of wrongs" (I Corinthians 13:5).
2. Each student chooses a blank thank you note from the basket to be used later in class.

Thank you for leading your team.

"Meet Oops"
Pop Quiz

1.

2.

3.

4.

5.

6.

7.

8.

9.

10.

11.

12.

13.

14.

15.

16.

17.

18.

Place Cards

Formal - plain, bordered, or monogrammed in gold or silver with title and last name.

Informal - decorative with first or first and last name.

Place Cards

Formal - plain, bordered, or monogrammed in gold or silver with title and last name.

Informal - decorative with first or first and last name.

Place Cards

Formal - plain, bordered, or monogrammed in gold or silver with title and last name.

Informal - decorative with first or first and last name.

Place Cards

Formal - plain, bordered, or monogrammed in gold or silver with title and last name.

Informal - decorative with first or first and last name.

Good Manners Report Card

_____'s

good manners were showing.
He or she was seen:

_____

_____

_____

_____

_____

Signed:

_____

Date:_____

Good Manners Report Card

_____'s

good manners were showing.
He or she was seen:

_____

_____

_____

_____

_____

Signed:

_____

Date:_____

Good Manners Report Card

_____'s

good manners were showing.
He or she was seen:

_____

_____

_____

_____

_____

Signed:

_____

Date:_____

Good Manners Report Card

_____'s

good manners were showing.
He or she was seen:

_____

_____

_____

_____

_____

Signed:

_____

Date:_____

Oops,
Your
Manners
Are
Showing™

Dear Teacher,

Please help us encourage good manners. Some of your students are enrolled in the manners class. Please refer to the list of names.

Use the attached forms to report the good manners of these students throughout the course (date   ). The reports will be read aloud in class and points awarded.

Thank you for supporting good manners.

Please take the forms to:

If you have any questions, please call:

Dear Parent,

GOOD MANNERS REPORT CARDS

Please complete the attached card to report the good manners you observe in your child.

Please send this card to class with your child. All cards will be read aloud and points awarded. A new card will be sent home each time one is returned.

Thank you for encouraging good manners.

News Article

Each student is asked to bring a news article for the next class (_____ Date _____). This article should be about a topic of interest to the student and appropriate for group discussion. It is helpful for the student to review the article before class to practice the lesson on conversation.

Points will be awarded for bringing the article.

Thank you,
Oops's class

Oops

Maddie Oopsman

Mamaw

Mark Oopsman

Paul Lite

Hank Yu

Alexandria Hamilton

Eddie Kit

Heloise Hamilton

Dr. Spleen

Rudy

Harold Hamilton

Coach Freestyle

Rose Valentine

Mrs. Stagemaster

Governor Powers

Joy Givens

Minnie Frenz

Reverend Divine

Oops's Birthday Punch

1 - 12 oz. can frozen
Pink Lemonade

1 - 46 oz. can Pineapple Juice

1 - 2 liter bottle of Gingerale,
Sprite, or 7up

Serves 20 - 6 oz. cups

Oops's Birthday Punch

1 - 12 oz. can frozen
Pink Lemonade

1 - 46 oz. can Pineapple Juice

1 - 2 liter bottle of Gingerale,
Sprite, or 7up

Serves 20 - 6 oz. cups

Oops's Birthday Punch

1 - 12 oz. can frozen
Pink Lemonade

1 - 46 oz. can Pineapple Juice

1 - 2 liter bottle of Gingerale,
Sprite, or 7up

Serves 20 - 6 oz. cups

Oops's Birthday Punch

1 - 12 oz. can frozen
Pink Lemonade

1 - 46 oz. can Pineapple Juice

1 - 2 liter bottle of Gingerale,
Sprite, or 7up

Serves 20 - 6 oz. cups

Oops's Birthday Punch

1 - 12 oz. can frozen
Pink Lemonade

1 - 46 oz. can Pineapple Juice

1 - 2 liter bottle of Gingerale,
Sprite, or 7up

Serves 20 - 6 oz. cups

Oops's Birthday Punch

1 - 12 oz. can frozen
Pink Lemonade

1 - 46 oz. can Pineapple Juice

1 - 2 liter bottle of Gingerale,
Sprite, or 7up

Serves 20 - 6 oz. cups

Oops's Birthday Punch

1 - 12 oz. can frozen
Pink Lemonade

1 - 46 oz. can Pineapple Juice

1 - 2 liter bottle of Gingerale,
Sprite, or 7up

Serves 20 - 6 oz. cups

Oops's Birthday Punch

1 - 12 oz. can frozen
Pink Lemonade

1 - 46 oz. can Pineapple Juice

1 - 2 liter bottle of Gingerale,
Sprite, or 7up

Serves 20 - 6 oz. cups

Dear Parent,

Please send a canned or packaged food for the next class
(Date   ). Students will use the food to
learn about table manners and then have the opportunity to
donate the cans to a food bank. Students will earn points for
bringing the food.

Thank you,

Oops's Class

Dear Parent,

Please send a canned or packaged food for the next class
(Date   ). Students will use the food to
learn about table manners and then have the opportunity to
donate the cans to a food bank. Students will earn points for
bringing the food.

Thank you,

Oops's Class

Please don't close the book on manners.

Dear Parent,

Our time of teaching manners with your child has almost come to an end. It is only the beginning, however, for your child to practice the lessons of good manners.

The student workbook is designed for continued use. Every time there is a party, a sports activity, or a thank you note to write, and maybe every time the telephone rings, please encourage your child to remember the manners workbook. It provides reminders and incentives.

Whenever good manners are showing, write about them and include your comments in the workbook. Every time someone in your family reads an article relating to manners, discuss it with your child and ask that it be added to the student folder.

Your child has expressed creativity in designing the illustration page. The contents of the workbook and folder can be claimed for a lifetime.

Thank you for allowing your child to learn with us during this course.

Oops, You're a Winner

This certifies that

has successfully completed the

Manners Class

_____
Date

_____
Signature

_____
Signature

He who began a good work in you will carry it on to completion until the day of Christ Jesus. Philippians 1:6b

Thank You

Thank You

"JUST DESSERTS CAFE"

Job Descriptions

Preparation - Make a copy of this sheet. Cut out each job description and give the description to the student filling the position. For four positions, combine the "Captain" and the *"maitre d'."* Create roles for more students such as another server or a bus boy or girl. *One or a few students perform more than one job.*

Maitre d'
1. Show guests to their seats.
2. Pull out chairs for ladies.
3. Give a menu to each guest.
4. Take your break, choose your dessert, & eat the dessert.

Captain
1. Go to the table after guests are seated, & say, "Welcome to the 'Just Desserts Cafe.'"
   "Your server will be with you in just-a-moment."
   "Our Dessert of the Day is:
   _____."
2. Assist in kitchen as needed.
3. Ask guests, "Are the desserts to your satisfaction?"
4. Take your break, choose your dessert, & eat the dessert.

Beverage Steward
1. After guests are seated, take their drink orders.
2. Give the chef your orders.
3. Take two drinks at a time.
4. Stand between two guests or serve to each guest's right.
5. Take your break, choose your dessert, & eat the dessert.

Chef
1. Fill orders.
2. Take your break, choose your dessert, & eat the dessert.

Server
1. Ask each guest, "May I take your dessert order."
   Dessert of the Day is:

   _____
2. Pick up menus.
3. Tell chef your orders.
4. Take two desserts at a time.
5. Stand between two guests or serve to each guest's left.
6. Take your break, choose your dessert, and eat the dessert.

Just Desserts Cafe
"Desserts Is Our Middle Name"

Pies

Just Good Ole American Apple Pie

Just Simply Delicious Cherry Pie

Just Pie of the Day

Drinks

Cola   Diet Cola   Uncola

Just Water

Just Desserts Cafe
Dessert Order Form

	Number	Whipped cream
Apple Pie	_____	_____
Cherry Pie	_____	_____
Pie of the Day	_____	_____

Just Desserts Cafe
Beverage Order Form

	Number
Cola	_____
Diet Cola	_____
Uncola	_____
Water	_____

Whoever serves me must follow me; and where I am, my servant also will be. My father will honor the one who serves me.

John 12:26

Notes . . .